Becoming a U.S. Citizen:

Understanding the Naturalization Process

Dene record

BECOMING A U.S. CITIZEN

UNDERSTANDING THE NATURALIZATION PROCESS

PUBLISHING

New York • Chicago

Editorial Director: Jennifer Farthing
Senior Editor: Ruth Baygell
Production Editor: David Shaw
Production Artist: Ellen Gurak
Cover Designer: Carly Schnur

Published by Kaplan Publishing, a division of Kaplan, Inc.
888 Seventh Ave.
New York, NY 10106

Printed in the United States of America

October 2006
10 9 8 7 6 5 4 3 2 1

Library of Congress Cataloging-in-Publication Data

Becoming a us citizen : understanding the naturalization process / by Kaplan, Inc.
    p.cm.
  ISBN-13: 978-1-4195-4199-5
  ISBN-10:   1-4195-4199-4
  1. Naturalization—United States—Popular works. 2. Citizenship—United States—Popular works.
  3. Citizenship—United States—Examinations, questions, etc. I. Kaplan, Inc. II. Title: Becoming a U.S. citizen.
  III. title: Becoming a United States citizen.
  KF4710.Z9B43 2006
  342.7308'3—dc22   2006020336

Kaplan Publishing books are available at special quantity discounts to use for sales promotions, employee premiums, or educational purposes. Please call our Special Sales Department to order or for more information at 800-621-9621, ext. 4444, email kaplanpubsales@kaplan.com, or write to Kaplan Publishing, 30 South Wacker Drive, Suite 2500, Chicago, IL 60606-7481.

Table of Contents

Step 5: Take the English Communication Practice Test

Step 6: Take the Civics Practice Test

How to Use This Book

Congratulations! You have made the decision to become a United States citizen. You may be at the point where you have a copy of Form N-400, the Application for Naturalization, from the U.S. Citizenship and Immigration Services (USCIS), or maybe you do not know where to start.

The naturalization process takes time and effort. You need to get the application, fill it out, and send it to the correct office with all of the necessary documents. Then you need to wait for a response, study for the English and Civics tests, be fingerprinted, and have your picture taken—and that's before you go for your interview!

The purpose of this book is to explain each step of the process as simply as possible, guiding you as you make your way from applicant to citizen. However, you may come across words that you are not familiar with. Do not skip them and hope you will figure them out later; some of those words could make the difference between understanding what you need to do and making a mistake. It is very important that you take the time to look those words up in a dictionary, and write down the definitions to study later.

In addition, do not be tempted to skip any of the practice exercises. They are designed to show you what to expect during the interview and to teach you how to pass the English and Civics tests and the interview itself. The tests in Steps 5 and 6 will reinforce what you learned in previous steps.

From time to time the USCIS makes changes in parts of the naturalization process. If you have questions it is a good idea to check the USCIS website (www.uscis.gov) or to call them at 1-800-375-5283. The USCIS publishes the helpful A Guide to the Naturalization Process that you can order or download from the website.

The decision to become a U.S. citizen is an important one. This book will guide you through the process, from application to oath ceremony to citizenship. Good luck!

Step 1: Understanding Citizenship, Naturalization, and Eligibility

Before you begin the naturalization process, you need to understand it. Why should you become a naturalized citizen? How does the naturalization process work? Who can and cannot become a naturalized citizen? This section helps you take the first step; it gives you the answers to these important questions and more.

WHAT IS CITIZENSHIP?

Citizenship refers to the legal status of being a citizen. It differs from being an alien or a national in that citizenship status gives a person more rights within the United States. In addition to those rights, citizenship also comes with responsibilities.

Rights of U.S. citizens include:

- The right to vote

- The right to have a U.S. passport

- The right to obtain a federal government job

- The right to have U.S. government protection and help when traveling to other countries

- The right to petition the U.S. government to allow close relatives to come to America to live

Responsibilities of citizenship include:

- Giving up allegiances to other countries

- Supporting and defending the Constitution and U.S. laws

- Swearing allegiance to the United States

- Serving in the armed forces of the United States when required

- Registering to vote

- Voting

- Serving on a jury

- Tolerating the differences of other citizens

HOW CAN YOU BECOME A U.S. CITIZEN?

There are two ways to become a citizen: by birth and through the naturalization process.

You are a U.S. citizen by birth if you were born in the United States or born to U.S. citizens (even if you were born outside the country). If one parent is a U.S. citizen and that parent lived at least five years in the United States before you were born and at least two of those years were after his or her 14th birthday, you are born a U.S. citizen. People born in Puerto Rico, Guam, and the U.S. Virgin Islands are also citizens by birth.

If you were not born an American citizen, you must go through the naturalization process to become one. If you are 18 or older, you must apply for naturalization using Form N-400, Application for Naturalization. This book explains every step of the naturalization process, from requesting Form N-400 and filling it out, to studying for the English and Civics tests.

ARE YOU ELIGIBLE FOR CITIZENSHIP VIA NATURALIZATION?

The naturalization process is open to most people who want to become citizens. Some of these people are already permanent residents, some are married to U.S. citizens, and others are serving or have served in the U.S. military. To be eligible for naturalization, these different groups must meet certain requirements.

General Requirements

No matter whether an applicant is in the military, works for an American company, is a permanent resident, or any other circumstance, everyone applying for naturalization must meet general requirements (although the details of those requirements may vary). Applicants must be at least 18 years old, and most must be permanent residents who have lived in the United States for a period of time, known as "continuous residence" and "physical presence" (see box below). In addition, most applicants must live in one district or state for a period of time (typically three months).

> **WHAT'S THE DIFFERENCE BETWEEN CONTINUOUS RESIDENCE AND PHYSICAL PRESENCE?**
>
> The continuous residence requirement refers to the number of days as a permanent resident that has not been broken by a trip of more than six months outside the United States. The physical presence requirement refers to the total number of days spent in the United States as a permanent resident.
>
> It is possible to meet the continuous residence requirement but not the physical presence requirement. This could happen if an applicant takes so many shorter trips (less than six months each) that he or she is not in the United States for the number of days needed.

Every applicant must possess good moral character, which means he or she does not have a serious criminal record. There are no exceptions to this requirement. Applicants must also be willing to pledge an oath of allegiance to the United States and its Constitution. Other requirements include knowledge of U.S. history and its system of government (known together as "civics"); and the ability to write, read, and speak basic English.

WHAT IS A PERMANENT RESIDENT? ————————

Once you enter the United States, you are not legally allowed to live and work in the country until you apply for and receive an immigrant visa (also called a "green card"). Immigrants with visas are known as permanent residents. Most people who apply for visas must have either a family member (who is already a U.S. citizen or permanent resident) or an employer sponsor them. For those without a sponsor, there is a green card "lottery." For more information about permanent resident status, check the website of the United States Citizenship and Immigration Services, www.uscis.gov.

For Permanent Residents

Most people applying for naturalization are permanent residents who have been so for at least five years and have no special circumstances. For these applicants, the requirements are:

- Continuous residence—At least five years with no trips outside the United States lasting six months or longer

- Physical presence—30 months

- Time in district or state—Three months

- English and Civics tests—Required

- Oath of allegiance—Required

If you have been married to and living with an American citizen for at least three years, and your spouse has been an American citizen for those three years, you must meet these requirements:

- Continuous residence—At least three years with no trips outside the United States lasting six months or longer

- Physical presence—18 months

- Time in district or state—Three months

- English and Civics tests—Required

- Oath of allegiance—Required

For Members, Employees, and Family Members of the Military

If you are in the U.S. Armed Forces (or were honorably discharged no longer than six months before filing your application) and have served for at least one year, you must be a permanent resident on the day of your interview. However, you do not need to meet requirements for continuous residence, physical presence, or time in district or state.

If you were honorably discharged more than six months ago, or served less than a year, your requirements are:

- Continuous residence—Five years as a permanent resident with no trips longer than six months (service overseas does not break the period of continuous residence)

- Physical presence—30 months (time spent in service overseas is included)

- Time in district or state—Three months

- English and Civics tests—Required

- Oath of allegiance—Required

If you performed active duty military service during a war (see box below), you do not have to be a permanent resident (unless you did not enlist or re-enlist in the United States or its outlying possessions). There are also no requirements for continuous residence, physical presence, or time in district or state. However, you must pass the English and Civics tests and take the oath of allegiance.

- World War I (November 11, 1916–April 6, 1917) ————
- World War II (September 1, 1939–December 31, 1946)
- Korea (June 25, 1950–July 1, 1955)
- Vietnam (February 28, 1961–October 15, 1978)
- Persian Gulf (August 2, 1990–April 11, 1991)
- On or after September 11, 2001

If you were married to a U.S. citizen who died during a period of honorable active duty service in the U.S. Armed Forces, and were married to and living with your spouse when he or she died, you must be a permanent resident on the day of your interview. There are no requirements for continuous residence, physical presence, or time in district or state, but you must pass the English and Civics tests and take the oath of allegiance.

If you served on a vessel operated by the United States or on a vessel registered in the United States and owned by U.S. citizens or a U.S. corporation, you must meet the following requirements:

- Continuous residence—Five years as a permanent resident with no trips outside the United States longer than six months (time spent in service is treated as time spent inside the United States)

- Physical presence—30 months (time spent in service is treated as time spent inside the United States)

- Time in district or state—Three months

- English and Civics tests—Required

- Oath of allegiance—Required

If you are an employee or an individual under contract to the U.S. government, your requirements are:

- Continuous residence—Five years as a permanent resident without leaving the United States for six months or longer (an absence for one year or more breaks continuous residence; maintaining continuous residence requires at least one year of unbroken continuous residence since becoming a permanent resident and an approved Application to Preserve Residence for Naturalization Purposes [Form N-470] before leaving the United States for a year)

- Physical presence—30 months (time spent outside the United States during this type of employment is considered time inside the United States as long as an N-470 is approved before leaving the United States for a year)

- Time in district or state—Three months

- English and Civics tests—Required

- Oath of allegiance—Required

Other Special Considerations

There are several other exceptions to the general rules for naturalization, including special requirements for U.S. nationals, members of the clergy, employees of American companies, and spouses of American citizens in certain professions. Your age and/or disability may also play a role in determining what requirements you must meet to become a citizen.

U.S. Nationals

If you are a U.S. national (a noncitizen who owes permanent allegiance to the United States), are a resident of any state, and are otherwise qualified for naturalization, you do not need to have permanent resident status. However, you must fulfill continuous residence, physical presence, and time in district or state requirements. You must also pass the English and Civics tests and take the oath of allegiance.

Clergy Members

If you perform ministerial or priestly functions for a religious denomination or an interdenominational organization with a valid presence in the United States, you must fulfill the following requirements:

- Continuous residence—Five years as a permanent resident without leaving the United States for trips of six months or longer (an absence for one year or more breaks continuous residence; maintaining continuous residence requires at least one year of unbroken continuous residence since becoming a permanent resident and an approved N-470 before leaving the United States for a year)

- Physical presence—30 months (time spent in this type of employment is considered time physically present in the United States if you get an approved N-470 before applying for naturalization)

- Time in district or state—Three months

- English and Civics tests—Required

- Oath of allegiance—Required

Employees of U.S. Companies or Institutions

If you are an employee of an American institution of research recognized by the attorney general, an American-owned firm or corporation engaged in the development of foreign trade and commerce for the United States, or a public international organization of which the United States is a member by law or treaty (if the employment began after you became a permanent resident), you must meet these requirements:

- Continuous residence—Five years as a permanent resident without leaving the United States for six months or longer (an absence for one year or more breaks continuous residence; maintaining continuous residence requires at least one year of unbroken continuous residence since becoming a permanent resident and an approved N-470 before leaving the United States for a year)

- Physical presence—30 months

- Time in district or state—Three months

- English and Civics tests—Required

- Oath of allegiance—Required

If you are an employee of a U.S. nonprofit organization that principally promotes the interests of the United States abroad through the communications media, and have been for at least five years, there are no requirements for continuous residence, physical presence, or time in district or state. However, you must pass the English and Civics tests and take the oath of allegiance.

Spouses of U.S. Citizens with Special Considerations

You must be a permanent resident, pass the English and Civics tests, and take the oath of allegiance, but you do not have to meet requirements for continuous residence, physical presence, or time in district or state if your spouse is a U.S. citizen working abroad under an employment contract with a qualifying employer from the following list for at least a year and will continue to work for that employer at the time you are naturalized. To qualify, your spouse must be

- a member of the U.S. Armed Forces;

- an employee or individual under contract to the U.S. government;

- an employee of an American research institution recognized by the attorney general;

- an employee of an American-owned firm or corporation that works to develop foreign trade and commerce for the United States;

- an employee of a public international organization of which the United States is a member by law or treaty; or

- a person who performs ministerial or priestly functions for a religious denomination or an interdenominational organization with a valid presence in the United States.

Exceptions for Age and Disabilities

If you are over the age of 50 and have lived in the United States as a permanent resident for 20 years or more, or are over the age of 55 and have lived in the United States as a permanent resident for at least 15 years, you must meet requirements for continuous residence, physical presence, and time in district or state. However, you can take the Civics test in the language of your choice, and you do not have to take the English test.

If you are over 65 and have lived in the United States as a permanent resident for at least 20 years, you must meet requirements for continuous residence, physical presence, and time in district or state. You may take an easier version of the Civics test in the language of your choice, and do not have to take the English test.

If you have a physical, developmental, or mental disability or impairment, you can apply for an exception to the English and Civics requirements by filing Form N-648, Medical Certification for Disability Exceptions, with your application.

I'M CONFUSED. WHO CAN ANSWER MY QUESTIONS? ──────

If you need help as you go through the naturalization process, check the following:

- USCIS website—The USCIS website (www.uscis.gov) explains how to become a citizen and offers *A Guide to Naturalization Process* and Form N-400 to download.

- Local USCIS office—There is an information counter at every USCIS office where an employee is available to answer your questions.

- USCIS National Customer Service Center—Call 1-800-375-5283 if you live in the continental United States for basic information about the naturalization process. You can order forms, find out the status of an application, and get advice before you file an application.

- Community-based organizations (CBOs)—There are many groups across the country that work to help people who want to become citizens. They help immigrants learn English and U.S. history and offer help filling out Form N-400. Some CBOs reach out to immigrants of specific races or ethnic backgrounds (such as those listed in the Congressional Hispanic Caucus Institute's Regional and Local Hispanic Organization Directory at www.chci.org/publications/pdf/directory/regional_orgs-1.pdf), and others are smaller and more local and help whoever is in need. To find a CBO, check the phonebook under "Immigration and Naturalization" or search the Internet. Other immigrants can also be a good source of information.

- Immigration lawyers—Lawyers who specialize in immigration law can answer your questions about eligibility and other issues. You may be able to find an immigration lawyer in your local phonebook; check under "Lawyer" or "Attorney," and under "Immigration and Naturalization." The American Immigration Law Foundation has an immigration lawyer referral service that can also help. Send an email to ilrs@aila.org or call 1-800-954-0254. They will give you the name of an attorney in your area who can help, and who will charge no more than $100 for a half-hour consultation.

NOTES

_____

_____

_____

_____

_____

_____

_____

_____

_____

_____

_____

_____

_____

_____

_____

_____

_____

_____

_____

_____

_____

_____

_____

_____

_____

_____

_____

_____

_____

_____

_____

_____

_____

_____

_____

_____

_____

_____

_____

_____

_____

_____

_____

_____

_____

_____

_____

_____

_____

_____

_____

_____

_____

_____

_____

_____

_____

_____

Step 2: **Applying for Naturalized Citizenship**

In this step, you learn everything you need to know to apply for citizenship, including how to fill out your application and how to prepare for your interview. Follow the directions carefully, and be sure to read over your application. If you make a mistake, the time it takes to process your application will be much longer than it needs to be.

When you have determined that you are eligible for citizenship, you need to get a copy of the application, called Form N-400. There are two ways to get N-400: You can call the USCIS and have them send a copy to you, or you can download the form from the Internet. The toll-free phone number for the USCIS is 1-800-870-3676, and their Internet address is www.uscis.gov.

FILLING OUT THE FORM

When you fill out the Form N-400 (Figure 2.1), complete each section. Do not leave anything blank, or the processing of your application will take longer. Answer everything honestly. All of the information on your application can be questioned during your interview. If the USCIS finds out that you did not tell the truth on your application or during your interview, your application will be denied.

PHOTOGRAPHS AND REQUIRED DOCUMENTS

After you complete your application, you need to have two color passport-style photographs taken of yourself. The photos must be full frontal, meaning you are looking straight at the camera. Your facial features and at least your right ear must be showing, even if your religion requires you to wear a head covering. Do not wear glasses or earrings. The photos must be identical, and must have your A-number written on the back. Your A-number is the eight-digit code beginning with the letter "A" that appears on your temporary resident card, permanent resident card, Homeland Security file, and other documents issued to you by the Department of Homeland Security. To see an example of an acceptable photo, check www.uscis. gov/graphics/publicaffairs/newsrels/04_08_02Photo_flyer.pdf or call the USCIS toll-free at 1-800-375-5283 to request a copy of the photo flyer.

In addition to two photographs, you must also send a copy of both sides of your permanent resident card (also called the alien registration receipt card or green card). If you have lost your card, send a copy of the receipt of your Form I-90, Application to Replace Alien Registration Receipt Card. Finally, include a check or money order for the application fee and the fingerprinting fee with your A-number written on the back.

If there is any part of the oath of allegiance (see page 41) that you cannot say because of religious beliefs or because a physical or mental disability prevents you from understanding it, you must include a letter with your application that explains your situation. For more information on modified oaths, see the section "The Loyalty Oath Ceremony" on page 41. Copies of other documents may be required for special circumstances. Read the following list carefully to determine whether any of the circumstances apply to you.

- If an attorney or accredited representative is acting on your behalf, send a completed original Form G-28, Notice of Entry of Appearance as Attorney or Representative.

- If your current legal name is different from the name on your permanent resident card, send the document(s) that legally changed your name (marriage certificate, divorce decree, or other court document).

Figure 2.1   Form N-400

OMB No. 1615-0052

N-400 Application
for Naturalization

Department of Homeland Security
U.S Citizenship and Immigration Services

Print clearly or type your answers using **CAPITAL** letters. Failure to print clearly may delay your application. Use black ink.

Part 1. Your Name. *(The Person Applying for Naturalization)*	Write your USCIS "A"- number here:
	A

A. Your current legal name.

Family Name *(Last Name)*

Given Name *(First Name)*   Full Middle Name *(If applicable)*

For USCIS Use Only

Bar Code	Date Stamp

B. Your name **exactly** as it appears on your Permanent Resident Card.

Family Name *(Last Name)*

Given Name *(First Name)*   Full Middle Name *(If applicable)*

Remarks

C. If you have ever used other names, provide them below.

Family Name *(Last Name)*	Given Name *(First Name)*	Middle Name

D. Name change *(optional)*

Please read the Instructions before you decide whether to change your name.

1. Would you like to legally change your name?   ☐ Yes   ☐ No

2. If "Yes," print the new name you would like to use. Do not use initials or abbreviations when writing your new name.

Family Name *(Last Name)*

Given Name *(First Name)*   Full Middle Name

Action Block

Part 2. Information About Your Eligibility. *(Check Only One)*

I am at least 18 years old **AND**

A. ☐ I have been a Lawful Permanent Resident of the United States for at least five years.

B. ☐ I have been a Lawful Permanent Resident of the United States for at least three years, **and** I have been married to and living with the same U.S. citizen for the last three years, **and** my spouse has been a U.S. citizen for the last three years.

C. ☐ I am applying on the basis of qualifying military service.

D. ☐ Other *(Please explain)* _____

Form N-400 (Rev. 10/26/05)Y

Source: www.uscis.gov

Figure 2.1   Form N-400 (continued)

Part 3. Information About You.	Write your USCIS "A"- number here: A

A. U.S. Social Security Number   **B.** Date of Birth *(mm/dd/yyyy)*   **C.** Date You Became a Permanent Resident *(mm/dd/yyyy)*

D. Country of Birth   **E.** Country of Nationality

F. Are either of your parents U.S. citizens? *(if yes, see Instructions)*   ☐ Yes   ☐ No

G. What is your current marital status?   ☐ Single, Never Married   ☐ Married   ☐ Divorced   ☐ Widowed

☐ Marriage Annulled or Other *(Explain)*

H. Are you requesting a waiver of the English and/or U.S. History and Government requirements based on a disability or impairment and attaching a Form N-648 with your application?   ☐ Yes   ☐ No

I. Are you requesting an accommodation to the naturalization process because of a disability or impairment? *(See Instructions for some examples of accommodations.)*   ☐ Yes   ☐ No

If you answered "Yes," check the box below that applies:

☐ I am deaf or hearing impaired and need a sign language interpreter who uses the following language:

☐ I use a wheelchair.

☐ I am blind or sight impaired.

☐ I will need another type of accommodation. Please explain:

Part 4. Addresses and Telephone Numbers.

A. Home Address - Street Number and Name *(Do **not** write a P.O. Box in this space)*   Apartment Number

City   County   State   ZIP Code   Country

B. Care of   Mailing Address - Street Number and Name *(If different from home address)*   Apartment Number

City   State   ZIP Code   Country

C. Daytime Phone Number *(If any)*   Evening Phone Number *(If any)*   E-mail Address *(If any)*

(   )   (   )

Figure 2.1   Form N-400 (continued)

Part 5. Information for Criminal Records Search.	Write your USCIS "A"- number here: A

NOTE: The categories below are those required by the FBI. See Instructions for more information.

A. Gender

☐ Male   ☐ Female

B. Height

Feet	Inches

C. Weight

Pounds

D. Are you Hispanic or Latino?   ☐ Yes   ☐ No

E. Race *(Select one or more.)*

☐ White   ☐ Asian   ☐ Black or African American   ☐ American Indian or Alaskan Native   ☐ Native Hawaiian or Other Pacific Islander

F. Hair color

☐ Black   ☐ Brown   ☐ Blonde   ☐ Gray   ☐ White   ☐ Red   ☐ Sandy   ☐ Bald (No Hair)

G. Eye color

☐ Brown   ☐ Blue   ☐ Green   ☐ Hazel   ☐ Gray   ☐ Black   ☐ Pink   ☐ Maroon   ☐ Other

Part 6. Information About Your Residence and Employment.

A. Where have you lived during the last five years? Begin with where you live now and then list every place you lived for the last five years. If you need more space, use a separate sheet(s) of paper.

Street Number and Name, Apartment Number, City, State, Zip Code and Country	Dates *(mm/dd/yyyy)*	
	From	To
Current Home Address - Same as Part 4.A		Present

B. Where have you worked (or, if you were a student, what schools did you attend) during the last five years? Include military service. Begin with your current or latest employer and then list every place you have worked or studied for the last five years. If you need more space, use a separate sheet of paper.

Employer or School Name	Employer or School Address *(Street, City and State)*	Dates *(mm/dd/yyyy)*		Your Occupation
		From	To	

Form N-400 (Rev. 10/26/05)Y Page 3

Figure 2.1 Form N-400 (continued)

Part 7. Time Outside the United States. *(Including Trips to Canada, Mexico and the Caribbean Islands)*	Write your USCIS "A"- number here: A

A. How many total days did you spend outside of the United States during the past five years?   [   ] days

B. How many trips of 24 hours or more have you taken outside of the United States during the past five years?   [   ] trips

C. List below all the trips of 24 hours or more that you have taken outside of the United States since becoming a Lawful Permanent Resident. Begin with your most recent trip. If you need more space, use a separate sheet(s) of paper.

Date You Left the United States *(mm/dd/yyyy)*	Date You Returned to the United States *(mm/dd/yyyy)*	Did Trip Last Six Months or More?	Countries to Which You Traveled	Total Days Out of the United States
		☐ Yes ☐ No		
		☐ Yes ☐ No		
		☐ Yes ☐ No		
		☐ Yes ☐ No		
		☐ Yes ☐ No		
		☐ Yes ☐ No		
		☐ Yes ☐ No		
		☐ Yes ☐ No		
		☐ Yes ☐ No		
		☐ Yes ☐ No		

Part 8. Information About Your Marital History.

A. How many times have you been married (including annulled marriages)?   [   ]   If you have **never** been married, go to Part 9.

B. If you are now married, give the following information about your spouse:

1. Spouse's Family Name *(Last Name)*   Given Name *(First Name)*   Full Middle Name *(If applicable)*

2. Date of Birth *(mm/dd/yyyy)*   **3.** Date of Marriage *(mm/dd/yyyy)*   **4.** Spouse's U.S. Social Security #

5. Home Address - Street Number and Name   Apartment Number

City   State   Zip Code

Figure 2.1   Form N-400 (continued)

Part 8. Information About Your Marital History.*(Continued)*	Write your USCIS "A"- number here: A

C. Is your spouse a U.S. citizen?   ☐ Yes   ☐ No

D. If your spouse is a U.S. citizen, give the following information:

    1. When did your spouse become a U.S. citizen?   ☐ At Birth   ☐ Other

    If "Other," give the following information:

    2. Date your spouse became a U.S. citizen

    3. Place your spouse became a U.S. citizen *(Please see Instructions)*

    City and State

E. If your spouse is **not** a U.S. citizen, give the following information :

    1. Spouse's Country of Citizenship

    2. Spouse's USCIS "A"- Number *(If applicable)*   A

    3. Spouse's Immigration Status

    ☐ Lawful Permanent Resident   ☐ Other

F. If you were married before, provide the following information about your prior spouse. If you have more than one previous marriage, use a separate sheet(s) of paper to provide the information requested in Questions 1-5 below.

    1. Prior Spouse's Family Name *(Last Name)*   Given Name *(First Name)*   Full Middle Name *(If applicable)*

    2. Prior Spouse's Immigration Status
    ☐ U.S. Citizen
    ☐ Lawful Permanent Resident
    ☐ Other

    3. Date of Marriage *(mm/dd/yyyy)*

    4. Date Marriage Ended *(mm/dd/yyyy)*

    5. How Marriage Ended
    ☐ Divorce   ☐ Spouse Died   ☐ Other

G. How many times has your current spouse been married (including annulled marriages)? ☐

    If your spouse has **ever** been married before, give the following information about **your spouse's** prior marriage.
    If your spouse has more than one previous marriage, use a separate sheet(s) of paper to provide the information requested in Questions 1 - 5 below.

    1. Prior Spouse's Family Name *(Last Name)*   Given Name *(First Name)*   Full Middle Name *(If applicable)*

    2. Prior Spouse's Immigration Status
    ☐ U.S. Citizen
    ☐ Lawful Permanent Resident
    ☐ Other

    3. Date of Marriage *(mm/dd/yyyy)*

    4. Date Marriage Ended *(mm/dd/yyyy)*

    5. How Marriage Ended
    ☐ Divorce   ☐ Spouse Died   ☐ Other

Form N-400 (Rev. 10/26/05)Y Page 5

KAPLAN

Figure 2.1   Form N-400 (continued)

Part 9. Information About Your Children.	Write your USCIS "A"- number here: A

A. How many sons and daughters have you had? For more information on which sons and daughters you should include and how to complete this section, see the Instructions.

B. Provide the following information about all of your sons and daughters. If you need more space, use a separate sheet(s) of paper.

Full Name of Son or Daughter	Date of Birth *(mm/dd/yyyy)*	USCIS "A"- number *(if child has one)*	Country of Birth	Current Address *(Street, City, State and Country)*
		A		
		A		
		A		
		A		
		A		
		A		
		A		
		A		

[Add Children]   [Go to continuation page]

Part 10. Additional Questions.

Please answer Questions 1 through 14. If you answer "Yes" to any of these questions, include a written explanation with this form. Your written explanation should (1) explain why your answer was "Yes" and (2) provide any additional information that helps to explain your answer.

A. General Questions.

1. Have you **ever** claimed to be a U.S. citizen *(in writing or any other way)*?   ☐ Yes   ☐ No

2. Have you **ever** registered to vote in any Federal, state or local election in the United States?   ☐ Yes   ☐ No

3. Have you **ever** voted in any Federal, state or local election in the United States?   ☐ Yes   ☐ No

4. Since becoming a Lawful Permanent Resident, have you **ever** failed to file a required Federal state or local tax return?   ☐ Yes   ☐ No

5. Do you owe any Federal, state or local taxes that are overdue?   ☐ Yes   ☐ No

6. Do you have any title of nobility in any foreign country?   ☐ Yes   ☐ No

7. Have you ever been declared legally incompetent or been confined to a mental institution within the last five years?   ☐ Yes   ☐ No

Form N-400 (Rev. 10/26/05)Y Page 6

Figure 2.1   Form N-400 (continued)

Part 10. Additional Questions. (Continued)	Write your USCIS "A"- number here: A

B. Affiliations.

8. a Have you **ever** been a member of or associated with any organization, association, fund foundation, party, club, society or similar group in the United States or in any other place?   ☐ Yes ☐ No

   b. If you answered "Yes," list the name of each group below. If you need more space, attach the names of the other group(s) on a separate sheet(s) of paper.

Name of Group	Name of Group
1.	6.
2.	7.
3.	8.
4.	9.
5.	10.

9. Have you **ever** been a member of or in any way associated *(either directly or indirectly)* with:

   a. The Communist Party?   ☐ Yes ☐ No

   b. Any other totalitarian party?   ☐ Yes ☐ No

   c. A terrorist organization?   ☐ Yes ☐ No

10. Have you **ever** advocated *(either directly or indirectly)* the overthrow of any government by force or violence?   ☐ Yes ☐ No

11. Have you **ever** persecuted *(either directly or indirectly)* any person because of race, religion, national origin, membership in a particular social group or political opinion?   ☐ Yes ☐ No

12. Between March 23, 1933 and May 8, 1945, did you work for or associate in any way *(either directly or indirectly)* with:

   a. The Nazi government of Germany?   ☐ Yes ☐ No

   b. Any government in any area (1) occupied by, (2) allied with, or (3) established with the help of the Nazi government of Germany?   ☐ Yes ☐ No

   c. Any German, Nazi, or S.S. military unit, paramilitary unit, self-defense unit, vigilante unit, citizen unit, police unit, government agency or office, extermination camp, concentration camp, prisoner of war camp, prison, labor camp or transit camp?   ☐ Yes ☐ No

C. Continuous Residence.

Since becoming a Lawful Permanent Resident of the United States:

13. Have you **ever** called yourself a "nonresident" on a Federal, state or local tax return?   ☐ Yes ☐ No

14. Have you **ever** failed to file a Federal, state or local tax return because you considered yourself to be a "nonresident"?   ☐ Yes ☐ No

Form N-400 (Rev.10/26/05) Y Page 7

KAPLAN

Figure 2.1   Form N-400 (continued)

Part 10. Additional Questions. (Continued)	Write your USCIS "A"- number here: A

D. Good Moral Character.

For the purposes of this application, you must answer "Yes" to the following questions, if applicable, even if your records were sealed or otherwise cleared or if anyone, including a judge, law enforcement officer or attorney, told you that you no longer have a record.

15. Have you **ever** committed a crime or offense for which you were **not** arrested? ☐ Yes ☐ No

16. Have you **ever** been arrested, cited or detained by any law enforcement officer (including USCIS or former INS and military officers) for any reason? ☐ Yes ☐ No

17. Have you **ever** been charged with committing any crime or offense? ☐ Yes ☐ No

18. Have you **ever** been convicted of a crime or offense? ☐ Yes ☐ No

19. Have you **ever** been placed in an alternative sentencing or a rehabilitative program (for example: diversion, deferred prosecution, withheld adjudication, deferred adjudication)? ☐ Yes ☐ No

20. Have you **ever** received a suspended sentence, been placed on probation or been paroled? ☐ Yes ☐ No

21. Have you **ever** been in jail or prison? ☐ Yes ☐ No

If you answered "Yes" to any of Questions 15 through 21, complete the following table. If you need more space, use a separate sheet(s) of paper to give the same information.

Why were you arrested, cited, detained or charged?	Date arrested, cited, detained or charged? *(mm/dd/yyyy)*	Where were you arrested, cited, detained or charged? *(City, State, Country)*	Outcome or disposition of the arrest, citation, detention or charge *(No charges filed, charges dismissed, jail, probation, etc.)*

Answer Questions 22 through 33. If you answer "Yes" to any of these questions, attach (1) your written explanation why your answer was "Yes" and (2) any additional information or documentation that helps explain your answer.

22. Have you **ever:**

   a. Been a habitual drunkard? ☐ Yes ☐ No

   b. Been a prostitute, or procured anyone for prostitution? ☐ Yes ☐ No

   c. Sold or smuggled controlled substances, illegal drugs or narcotics? ☐ Yes ☐ No

   d. Been married to more than one person at the same time? ☐ Yes ☐ No

   e. Helped anyone enter or try to enter the United States illegally? ☐ Yes ☐ No

   f. Gambled illegally or received income from illegal gambling? ☐ Yes ☐ No

   g. Failed to support your dependents or to pay alimony? ☐ Yes ☐ No

23. Have you **ever** given false or misleading information to any U.S. government official while applying for any immigration benefit or to prevent deportation, exclusion or removal? ☐ Yes ☐ No

24. Have you **ever** lied to any U.S. government official to gain entry or admission into the United States? ☐ Yes ☐ No

Figure 2.1   Form N-400 (continued)

Part 10. Additional Questions. (Continued)	Write your USCIS "A"- number here: A

E.   Removal, Exclusion and Deportation Proceedings.

25. Are removal, exclusion, rescission or deportation proceedings pending against you?   ☐ Yes   ☐ No

26. Have you **ever** been removed, excluded or deported from the United States?   ☐ Yes   ☐ No

27. Have you **ever** been ordered to be removed, excluded or deported from the United States?   ☐ Yes   ☐ No

28. Have you **ever** applied for any kind of relief from removal, exclusion or deportation?   ☐ Yes   ☐ No

F. Military Service.

29. Have you **ever** served in the U.S. Armed Forces?   ☐ Yes   ☐ No

30. Have you **ever** left the United States to avoid being drafted into the U.S. Armed Forces?   ☐ Yes   ☐ No

31. Have you **ever** applied for any kind of exemption from military service in the U.S. Armed Forces?   ☐ Yes   ☐ No

32. Have you **ever** deserted from the U.S. Armed Forces?   ☐ Yes   ☐ No

G. Selective Service Registration.

33. Are you a male who lived in the United States at any time between your 18th and 26th birthdays   ☐ Yes   ☐ No
in any status except as a lawful nonimmigrant?
If you answered "NO," go on to question 34.

If you answered "YES," provide the information below.

If you answered "YES," but you did not register with the Selective Service System and are still under 26 years of age, you
must register before you apply for naturalization, so that you can complete the information below:

Date Registered (mm/dd/yyyy) [   ]   Selective Service Number [   ]

If you answered "YES," but you did not register with the Selective Service and you are now 26 years old or older, attach a
statement explaining why you did not register.

H. Oath Requirements. *(See Part 14 for the Text of the Oath)*

Answer Questions 34 through 39. If you answer "No" to any of these questions, attach (1) your written explanation why the
answer was "No" and (2) any additional information or documentation that helps to explain your answer.

34. Do you support the Constitution and form of government of the United States?   ☐ Yes   ☐ No

35. Do you understand the full Oath of Allegiance to the United States?   ☐ Yes   ☐ No

36. Are you willing to take the full Oath of Allegiance to the United States?   ☐ Yes   ☐ No

37. If the law requires it, are you willing to bear arms on behalf of the United States?   ☐ Yes   ☐ No

38. If the law requires it, are you willing to perform noncombatant services in the U.S. Armed Forces?   ☐ Yes   ☐ No

39. If the law requires it, are you willing to perform work of national importance under civilian   ☐ Yes   ☐ No
direction?

Form N-400 (Rev. 10/26/05)Y Page 9

KAPLAN

Figure 2.1   Form N-400 (continued)

Part 11. Your Signature.	Write your USCIS "A"- number here: A

I certify, under penalty of perjury under the laws of the United States of America, that this application, and the evidence submitted with it, are all true and correct. I authorize the release of any information that the USCIS needs to determine my eligibility for naturalization.

Your Signature

Date *(mm/dd/yyyy)*

Part 12. Signature of Person Who Prepared This Application for You. *(If Applicable)*

I declare under penalty of perjury that I prepared this application at the request of the above person. The answers provided are based on information of which I have personal knowledge and/or were provided to me by the above named person in response to the *exact questions* contained on this form.

Preparer's Printed Name

Preparer's Signature

Date *(mm/dd/yyyy)*

Preparer's Firm or Organization Name *(If applicable)*

Preparer's Daytime Phone Number

Preparer's Address - Street Number and Name

City

State

Zip Code

NOTE: Do not complete Parts 13 and 14 until a USCIS Officer instructs you to do so.

Part 13. Signature at Interview.

I swear (affirm) and certify under penalty of perjury under the laws of the United States of America that I know that the contents of this application for naturalization subscribed by me, including corrections numbered 1 through _____ and the evidence submitted by me numbered pages 1 through _____ , are true and correct to the best of my knowledge and belief.

Subscribed to and sworn to (affirmed) before me

Officer's Printed Name or Stamp

Date *(mm/dd/yyyy)*

Complete Signature of Applicant

Officer's Signature

Part 14. Oath of Allegiance.

If your application is approved, you will be scheduled for a public oath ceremony at which time you will be required to take the following oath of allegiance immediately prior to becoming a naturalized citizen. By signing, you acknowledge your willingness and ability to take this oath:

I hereby declare, on oath, that I absolutely and entirely renounce and abjure all allegiance and fidelity to any foreign prince, potentate, state, or sovereignty, of whom or which I have heretofore been a subject or citizen;

that I will support and defend the Constitution and laws of the United States of America against all enemies, foreign and domestic;

that I will bear true faith and allegiance to the same;

that I will bear arms on behalf of the United States when required by the law;

that I will perform noncombatant service in the Armed Forces of the United States when required by the law;

that I will perform work of national importance under civilian direction when required by the law; and

that I take this obligation freely, without any mental reservation or purpose of evasion; so help me God.

Printed Name of Applicant

Complete Signature of Applicant

Form N-400 (Rev. 10/26/05)Y Page 10

If you are applying for naturalization on the basis of marriage to a U.S. citizen, send the following four things:

1. Evidence that your spouse has been a U.S. citizen for the last three years:

   - birth certificate (if your spouse never lost citizenship since birth);

   - naturalization certificate;

   - certificate of citizenship;

   - the inside of the front cover and signature page of your spouse's current U.S. passport; or

   - form FS240, Report of Birth Abroad of a Citizen of the United States of America

2. Your current marriage certificate

3. Proof of termination of all prior marriages of your spouse [divorce decree(s), annulment(s), or death certificate(s)]

4. Documents referring to you and your spouse:

   - tax returns, bank accounts, leases, mortgages, or birth certificates of children; or

   - Internal Revenue Service-certified copies of the income tax forms that you both filed for the past three years; or

   - an IRS tax return transcript for the last three years:

      - If you were married before, send proof that all earlier marriages ended [divorce decree(s), annulment(s), or death certificate(s)].

      - If you were previously in the U.S. military, send a completed original Form G-325B, Biographic Information.

- If you are currently in U.S. military service and are seeking citizenship based on that service, send a completed original Form N-426, Request for Certification of Military or Naval Service; and a completed original Form G-325B, Biographic Information.

- If you have taken any trip outside of the United States that lasted for six months or more since becoming a permanent resident, send evidence that you (and your family) continued to live, work, and/or keep ties to the United States, such as:

  - an IRS tax return "transcript" or an IRS-certified tax return listing tax information for the last five years (or for the last three years if you are applying on the basis of marriage to a U.S. citizen); or

  - rent or mortgage payments and pay stubs.

- If you have a dependent spouse or children who do not live with you, send

  1. any court or government order to provide financial support; and

  2. evidence of your financial support (including evidence that you have complied with any court or government order), such as:

     - cancelled checks;

     - money order receipts;

     - a court or agency printout of child support payments;

     - evidence of wage garnishments; or

     - a letter from the parent or guardian who cares for your children.

- If you answer "Yes" to any of questions 1 through 15 in Part 7, send a written explanation on a separate sheet of paper.

- If you answer "No" to any of questions 1 through 5 in Part 8, send a written explanation on a separate sheet of paper.

- If you have ever been arrested or detained by any law enforcement officer for any reason, and no charges were filed, send an original official statement by the arresting agency or applicable court confirming that no charges were filed.

- If you have ever been arrested or detained by any law enforcement officer for any reason, and charges were filed, send an original or court-certified copy of the complete arrest record and disposition for each incident (dismissal order, conviction record, or acquittal order).

- If you have ever been convicted or placed in an alternative sentencing program or rehabilitative program (such as a drug treatment or community service program), send an original or court-certified copy of the sentencing record for each incident, and evidence that you completed your sentence (an original or certified copy of your probation or parole record, or evidence that you completed an alternative sentencing program or rehabilitative program).

- If you have ever had any arrest or conviction vacated, set aside, sealed, expunged, or otherwise removed from your record, send an original or court-certified copy of the court order vacating, setting aside, sealing, expunging, or otherwise removing the arrest or conviction, or an original statement from the court that no record exists of your arrest or conviction.

- If you have ever failed to file an income tax return since you became a permanent resident, send all correspondence with the IRS regarding your failure to file.

- If you have any federal, state, or local taxes that are overdue, send a signed agreement from the IRS or state or local tax office showing that you have filed a tax return and arranged to pay the taxes you owe; and documentation from the IRS or state or local tax office showing the current status of your repayment program.

- If you are applying for a disability exception to the testing requirement, send an original Form N-648, Medical Certification for Disability Exceptions, completed less than six months ago by a licensed medical or osteopathic doctor or licensed clinical psychologist.

- If you did not register with the Selective Service and you are male, are 26 years old or older, and lived in the United States in a status other than as a lawful nonimmigrant between the ages of 18 and 26, send a Status Information Letter from the Selective Service (call 1-847-688-6888 for more information).

PROCESSING FEES

At the time of printing of this book, the fees for processing Form N-400 were $320 for filing and $70 for having fingerprints taken. The fingerprint fee is not required if you are 75 years old or older.

If you are filing from abroad, the USCIS will tell you where to have your fingerprints taken, and a fee will be collected at the time of the fingerprinting. The application fees are not refundable even if your case is denied or you withdraw your application.

Include a check or money order (not cash) for $390 ($320 if you are 75 years old or older or if you are filing from abroad) payable to the U.S. Department of Homeland Security. Write your A-number on the back of the check or money order.

If you are a resident of Guam, make the fee payable to the Treasurer, Guam. If you are a resident of the U.S. Virgin Islands, make the fee payable to the Commissioner of Finance of the Virgin Islands.

HOLD THAT ENVELOPE!

Before you seal your application in an envelope, make a copy of it. Why? During your interview with a USCIS officer, he or she asks you questions about your application, so it makes sense to review it before the interview—you can even bring it with you to the interview, but you can't use it to prepare if you mail your only copy.

WHERE TO SEND YOUR APPLICATION

When you have completed your application, and have your photographs, required documents, and fees ready, mail them to one of the following locations, depending on where you live.

If you live in:	Send your application to:
Arizona California Hawaii Nevada Territory of Guam The Commonwealth of the Northern Mariana Islands	California Service Center P.O. Box 10400 Laguna Niguel, California 2607-0400
If you live in:	**Send your application to:**
Alaska Colorado Idaho Illinois Indiana Iowa Kansas Michigan Minnesota Missouri Montana Nebraska North Dakota Ohio Oregon South Dakota Utah Washington Wisconsin Wyoming	Nebraska Service Center P.O. Box 87400 Lincoln, Nebraska 68501-7400

If you live in:	Send your application to:
Alabama Arkansas Florida Georgia Kentucky Louisiana Mississippi New Mexico North Carolina Oklahoma South Carolina Tennessee Texas	Texas Service Center P.O. Box 851204 Mesquite, Texas 75185-1204
If you live in:	**Send your application to:**
Connecticut District of Columbia Delaware Maine Maryland Massachusetts New Hampshire New Jersey New York Pennsylvania Rhode Island Vermont Virginia West Virginia Commonwealth of Puerto Rico U.S. Virgin Islands	Vermont Service Center 75 Lower Weldon Street St. Albans, Vermont 05479-0001

YOUR FINGERPRINTING APPOINTMENT

After you file your application, you will get a letter telling you when and where to have your fingerprints taken. Most fingerprints are taken at application support centers or police departments. If you do not live near a fingerprinting location, the USCIS may send a van to your area in which to take fingerprints. If you are filing from abroad, the USCIS directs you to a U.S. consular office to be fingerprinted.

On the day you are to have your fingerprints taken, bring the letter you received from the USCIS, your permanent resident card, and another form of identification with a picture on it (driver's license, passport, or state identification card).

When you arrive at the fingerprinting location, your documents are checked and your fingerprints taken, usually with ink. Some sites now use electronic technology to take the prints without ink, and eventually all sites will use this technology. Your fingerprints are then sent to the FBI for a criminal background check.

WHAT IT MEANS IF YOUR FINGERPRINTS ARE REJECTED

Sometimes the FBI rejects fingerprints because they are not clear enough to read. If this happens, the USCIS sends you a letter telling you when to go back to the fingerprinting site. You are not charged another fingerprinting fee. If the FBI rejects your fingerprints again, you may need to contact the police departments in every place you have lived during the past five years to get police clearances. These clearances tell the FBI that you did not commit any crimes.

WHAT TO EXPECT AT THE INTERVIEW

The USCIS notifies you by mail regarding when and where to go for your interview. It is therefore very important that the USCIS has your correct address; let them know any time your address changes. If you cannot get to the interview, write to the office where it is scheduled and ask for a new date. Because rescheduling can add many months to the naturalization process, it is best to go to the first scheduled interview. If you do reschedule, the USCIS mails you a new notice with the rescheduled date. If you do not reschedule, and do not go to the interview, your case is closed. You then have one year to write to the USCIS and ask that your case be reopened. If you wait longer than one year, you have to file a new application (and pay fees again) to restart the naturalization process.

On the day of your interview, bring your permanent resident card or alien registration card, your passport (even if expired), and re-entry permits if you have them. If you were asked in the interview letter to bring other documents, make sure you have them with you. If you do not bring all of the documents requested by the USCIS, your application could be delayed or denied.

BEING PLACED UNDER OATH

At the start of your interview, the USCIS officer asks you to swear or promise that everything you say is true. Once you make that promise, you are "under oath." If you tell the officer something that is not true when under oath, your application will be denied. Because the officer asks you questions about your application, it is very important to tell the truth on the application as well as in your interview. If the USCIS finds out that you have said or written something that is not true after you have become a citizen, they can take away your citizenship.

Get to the office early and let the person at the front desk know that you are there. When it is time for your interview, a USCIS officer checks your documents and asks you questions about your application. He or she wants to know where you are from, where you live, how long you have lived there, your moral character, and your willingness to take an oath of allegiance to the United States.

WHO CAN COME WITH YOU TO YOUR INTERVIEW?

If you do not have to meet the English requirements (you are over 50 years old and have lived in the United States as a permanent resident for at least 20 years; over 55 years old and have lived in the United States as a permanent resident for at least 15 years; or if you have a disability that qualifies as a medical exemption), you can bring an interpreter to your interview.

If you want to bring your attorney or another representative, you must send Form G-28, Notice of Entry of Appearance as Attorney or Representative, with your application.

If you have a disability, you can bring a family member or legal guardian.

If you do not have a disability and plan to take the English test, you may bring someone with you to the USCIS office, but that person is not allowed in the interview room. Because it is often crowded in USCIS offices, it is best to bring someone with you only if necessary.

THE ENGLISH AND CIVICS TESTS

Your interview tests your knowledge of English and Civics (U.S. history and government). Steps 3 and 4 explain everything you need to know to pass the English and Civics tests, including how the English and Civics tests are given. Study the steps carefully, and complete all of the practice exercises. Steps 5 and 6 provide more opportunities for practice, including English read-aloud exercises and questions based on Form N-400.

Some people may not have to take one or both tests because of age or disability. If you are over 50 years old and have lived in the United States as a permanent resident for at least 20 years, or are over 55 years old and have lived as a permanent resident for at least 15 years, you do not have to take the English test, but do have to take a Civics test in your own language. If you are over 65 years old and have been a permanent resident for at least 20 years, you receive a simpler Civics test in your choice of language.

People with some kinds of disabilities may be exempt from the English and Civics tests. To get this exemption, the applicant must file Form N-648, Medical Certification for Disability Exemptions. This form must be completed and signed by a doctor.

Sample English and Civics tests questions are as follows:

Read the following sentences out loud:

I want to become a citizen.

He lives on a nice street.

Answer the following questions out loud:

Who is the president of the United States?

What colors make up the American flag?

Choose the best answer to the following questions:

1. How many terms may a president serve?

    a. one

    b. four

    c. two

    d. no limit

2. What country did the Americans fight in the American Revolution?

    a. France

    b. Canada

    c. Germany

    d. England

STRATEGIES TO HELP YOU SUCCEED IN THE INTERVIEW

Many applicants view the interview as the most stressful part of the naturalization process. It doesn't have to be. Here are 10 tips to help you lessen the stress, and handle yourself well.

1. Get to the USCIS office early

   Traffic, bad directions, lack of parking spaces, and long lines for security checkpoints can make you late. Plan ahead; get as much information as possible. Where is the office? What entrance do you use? How long do most people have to wait to get into the building and inside the waiting room? Call ahead, visit the building, and talk with people who are familiar with your local USCIS office. Find out exactly when to leave your house. When you get there early, and know what to expect, you will be better able to relax.

2. Follow directions about the exact paperwork that you need to bring with you

   Bring the documents the USCIS requested, including your permanent resident or alien registration card, your passport (even if expired), and re-entry permits if you have them. If the interview letter asked you to bring other documents, make sure that you have them with you. If you do not bring all of the documents requested by the USCIS, your application could be delayed or denied.

3. Be positive and polite

   A positive attitude tells your interviewer that you are confident—confident in your own abilities and that the naturalization process will go well for you. Shake hands firmly, sit up straight in your chair, and make eye contact. Do not act superior. Treat everyone at the USCIS office with respect, including the person who takes your fingerprints.

4. Bring supporting documents

A copy of your application is useful when you are asked questions about what you answered on it. Other documents can show the USCIS officer that you have a home, have a job, and are active in your community. Bring papers such as the lease for your apartment, a letter from your employer, a copy of your latest pay stub or income tax return, proof of membership in organizations, or a thank-you note for volunteer work.

5. Dress to impress

You do not need to be formal, but a neat and clean appearance shows the USCIS officer that you are serious, and it gives a great first impression.

6. Be prepared for the questions you will be asked

Steps 3 and 4 explain exactly what you need to know and do to pass the English and Civics tests. Most people, including American citizens, do not know or remember all of the history and government facts that could be on the test. Spend time studying until you are familiar with all of them. Do all of the practice exercises, including those that help improve your English skills. When you are prepared, you are less nervous and better able to take the tests.

7. Ask for help if you need it

If you do not understand a question from the interviewer or something on a test, politely ask to have it explained to you.

8. Tell the truth

You already know how important it is that everything you say during your interview and everything you write on your application is the truth, but it's worth repeating: If the USCIS finds that something you said or wrote is not true, they can deny your application. If you are already a citizen and they find out about a lie, they can take your citizenship away. Telling the truth is absolutely necessary.

9. Do not make excuses

If there is something on your application that embarrasses you, such as a crime you committed or a divorce, answer any questions about it calmly and directly. Do not offer any new information about the incident unless it is specifically asked for. You may have made a mistake or two in the past, but the interviewer can still get a positive impression if you are likeable and appear to be of good character. Making excuses for past mistakes does not help.

10. Relax

It's not easy to be relaxed, but being prepared, having all the documents you need, looking neat and clean, and being on time can help.

WHAT IF I AM NOT TREATED FAIRLY? ─────────────

Most USCIS employees are professionals who treat everyone going through the naturalization process with respect. However, if you feel a USCIS employee did not treat you properly, you should speak with his or her direct supervisor. If you cannot speak with that person, write a letter to the director of your district office explaining the situation. The director should be able to resolve the issue.

Another way to make a complaint is by using Form I-847, Report of a Complaint, which can be ordered from the USCIS forms line at 1-800-870-3676. The form is a postcard with the address of USCIS headquarters printed on it.

THE APPLICATION DECISION

Some applicants find out at the end of their interview if they will be granted citizenship. Others must wait for a decision to come in the mail. Either way, the decision is either granted (accepted), continued (put on hold), or denied.

Granted

If your interview goes well and you pass the English and Civics tests, you are granted citizenship. Your interviewer may tell you the decision or you may leave the USCIS office without knowing. In the latter case, a notice is sent in the mail telling you of the decision, including when and where your oath ceremony will be. If you find out after your interview, you may be able to take the oath ceremony on the same day.

Continued

Your case is continued (put on hold) if you fail the English or Civics test (or both), or if you do not bring the correct documents to the interview. If you fail a test, you get a second interview date (typically 60–90 days after the first interview). If you fail again, your application is denied.

If you do not bring the necessary documents, you get Form N-14, which explains the documents you need to provide, and when and how to get those documents to the USCIS. Follow the directions on Form N-14 carefully—if you make a mistake, such as sending the wrong document, sending the right document to the wrong address, or sending the right document too late, your application may be denied.

Denied

The USCIS sends you a letter if your application is denied. In it, they tell you the reason for the denial and explain what you can do if you think the decision to deny is wrong. The notice includes Form N-336, Request for Hearing on a Decision in Naturalization Proceedings under Section 336 of the Act. To ask for a hearing with a USCIS officer, you need to fill out this form and file it within 30 days after you receive the denial letter. A fee (currently $265) is required with Form N-336. Send a check for that amount payable to Department of Homeland Security or U.S. Citizenship and Immigration Services.

After your appeal hearing, you are told whether your application is still denied. If it is, and you still believe your application should be granted, you can file a petition for a new review of your application in U.S. District Court.

THE LOYALTY OATH CEREMONY

If your application is granted, you must attend a loyalty oath ceremony. The ceremony may be held on the day of your interview or you will receive a Notice of Naturalization Oath Ceremony (Form N-445) that tells you the date and time of your ceremony. If you cannot attend the ceremony on the scheduled date, return Form N-445 to your local USCIS office with a letter explaining why you cannot attend and requesting a new date.

On the back of Form N-445 are questions the USCIS officer may ask you before the ceremony about things you may have done since your interview. These questions may include "Have you traveled outside the United States?" and "Have you claimed exemption from military service?" Write your answers to these questions on the back of the form, remembering to answer only about the time since your USCIS interview.

Whether you attend the ceremony on the same day as your interview or on another day, you must first check in with the USCIS and return your permanent resident card. As with your interview, the ceremony is crowded, so you should plan to arrive early. After everyone checks in, an official reads the oath slowly, one part at a time. You are asked to repeat his or her words.

THE OATH OF ALLEGIANCE ————————————————

I hereby declare, on oath, that I absolutely and entirely renounce and abjure all allegiance and fidelity to any foreign prince, potentate, state, or sovereignty of whom or which I have heretofore been a subject or citizen; that I will support and defend the Constitution and laws of the United States of America against all enemies, foreign and domestic; that I will bear true faith and allegiance to the same; that I will bear arms on behalf of the United States when required by the law; that I will perform noncombatant service in the armed forces of the United States when required by the law; that I will perform work of national importance under civilian direction when required by the law; and that I take this obligation freely without any mental reservation or purpose of evasion; so help me God.

You should note that in the oath you give up allegiance to the country of which you were formerly a citizen. Naturalization requirements also state that you must give up any hereditary title (such as Earl or Baron) or position of nobility you held in that country.

Some parts of the oath may be changed, or modified, for certain individuals. If you cannot say the entire oath for one of the following reasons, write a letter to the USCIS and include it with your application. The USCIS may ask you to bring to the interview or send a document from your religious organization that explains its beliefs and states that you are a member in good standing. If the document is accepted, you can take a modified oath.

The five possible modifications of the oath are:

1. If because of your religious beliefs you would not fight for the United States, you can take the oath without saying "to bear arms on behalf of the United States when required by law."

2. If because of your religious beliefs you would not serve in any way for the Armed Forces, you can take the oath without saying "to perform noncombatant service in the Armed Forces of the United States when required by law."

3. If you cannot swear the oath using the words "on oath," you may say instead "and solemnly affirm."

4. If your religious beliefs prevent you from saying "so help me God," you may leave those words out.

5. If you cannot understand the oath because of a physical or mental disability, you may be excused from the requirement.

After you take the oath, you get a Certificate of Naturalization. This paper is your proof of citizenship. If it is lost, destroyed, or stolen, or if you legally change your name, you need to apply for a replacement. Replacements can take up to one year to receive. During that year, you have no proof of citizenship unless you already have a U.S. passport. For this reason, it makes sense to apply for a passport as soon as you get your Certificate of Naturalization.

Applications for passports are sometimes available at loyalty oath ceremonies. You can also download one from the Internet (www.travel.state.gov/passport/forms/forms_847.html) or pick one up at a post office or passport acceptance facility. To find a facility near you, where you can get an application and apply for a passport, check www.iafdb.travel.state.gov/ or call the National Passport Information Center (NPIC) at 1-877-487-2778.

CHECKLIST: ARE YOU ELIGIBLE FOR NATURALIZATION?

This guide is designed to help you determine whether you are eligible to apply for and be granted naturalization status or not. It covers the situations of most applicants—those over 18 years of age who have been permanent residents for at least three years. Do not use this guide if you are under 18 years old, are not a permanent resident, and/or have not been a permanent resident for at least three years; you are not eligible to apply for naturalization. (There are a few exceptions for permanent residents 18 years old or over; see the section "Are You Eligible for Citizenship via Naturalization" in Step 1 for more details.)

If you answer all applicable questions and you are not told that your application will be denied, you are probably eligible to apply for naturalization. If you are told your application will be denied for a reason other than length of time in the United States or as a permanent resident, seek the advice of an immigration expert (see the box on page 9 in Step 1 to find out where you can get answers to your questions).

If you are 18 years old or older, and have been a permanent resident for at least five years, answer the following questions:

1. Have you been outside of the United States for 30 months or more?

If you answer "Yes"—Your application will be denied unless those 30 or more months were spent

- serving on board a vessel operated by or registered in the United States;

- working under contract to the U.S. government; or

- performing ministerial or priestly functions for a religious denomination or an interdenominational organization with a valid presence in the United States.

If one of the above exceptions applies to you, continue reading the rest of the questions.

If you answer "No"—Continue reading the rest of the questions to make sure that you are eligible to apply for naturalization.

2. Have you taken a trip outside the United States lasting one year or longer?

If you answer "Yes"—Your application will be denied. The exception to this rule is for those who

- served on board a vessel operated by or registered in the United States;

- worked under contract to the U.S. government; or

- performed ministerial or priestly functions for a religious denomination or an interdenominational organization with a valid presence in the United States.

If you are in one of these categories and you had an approved Form N-470, Application to Preserve Residence for Naturalization Purposes, before leaving the United States for a year or more, you can apply. Continue reading the rest of the questions.

If you answer "No"—Continue reading the rest of the questions to make sure that you are eligible to apply for naturalization.

3. Have you lived in the district or state where you are applying for naturalization for the last three months?

If you answer "Yes"—Continue reading the rest of the questions to make sure that you are eligible to apply for naturalization.

If you answer "No"—You must wait until you have lived there for three months before applying.

4. Can you read, write, and speak basic English? Do you know the history of the United States and its form of government?

If you answer "Yes"—Continue reading the rest of the questions to make sure that you are eligible to apply for naturalization.

If the answer "No"—Your application will be denied unless you meet one of the following exceptions:

- you are over age 50 and have been a permanent resident for at least 20 years;

- you are over age 55 and have been a permanent resident for at least 15 years;

- you are over age 65 and have been a permanent resident for at least 20 years; or

- you have a disability and are filing Form N-648, Medical Certification for Disability Exceptions.

If exceptions 1, 2, or 3 describe you, then you do not have to take the English test. People who meet the requirements for exceptions 1 and 2 must take the Civics test in the language of their choice. Those who meet exception 3 must take a simpler version of the Civics test in the language of their choice. If exception 4 describes you, you do not have to take the English or Civics test.

If you meet one of these four exceptions, continue reading the rest of the questions to make sure that you are eligible to apply for naturalization.

5. Do you have a serious criminal record?

If you answer "Yes"—Your application will be denied.

If you answer "No"—Continue reading the rest of the questions to make sure that you are eligible to apply for naturalization.

6. If you are male, are you registered with the Selective Service?

If you answer "Yes"—Continue reading the rest of the questions to make sure that you are eligible to apply for naturalization.

If you answer "No"—Unless you did not enter the United States before the age of 26, or entered between the ages of 18 and 26 and did not register but have a letter from the Selective Service explaining why, you must be registered or your application will be denied. If you meet these exceptions, continue reading the questions.

7. Have you deserted from the U.S. military?

If you answer "Yes"—Your application will be denied.

If you answer "No"—Continue reading the rest of the questions to make sure that you are eligible to apply for naturalization.

8. Have you received an exemption or discharge from the U.S. military because you are an alien?

> If you answer "Yes"—Your application will be denied.

> If you answer "No"—Continue reading the rest of the questions to make sure that you are eligible to apply for naturalization.

9. Are you willing to serve in the military or civilian service for the United States if the law requires you to do so?

> If you answer "Yes"—Continue reading the rest of the questions to make sure that you are eligible to apply for naturalization.

> If you answer "No "—Unless your religious beliefs or teaching prohibit it, you must be willing to serve or your application will be denied.

10. Will you support the U.S. Constitution?

> If you answer "Yes"—Continue reading the rest of the questions to make sure that you are eligible to apply for naturalization.

> If you answer "No"—Your application will be denied.

11. Do you understand the oath of allegiance to the United States (see page 41), and are you willing to take it?

> If you answer "Yes"—Read the rest of the questions to make sure that you are eligible to apply for naturalization.

> If you answer "No"—Your application will be denied.

If you are 18 years old or older, and have been a permanent resident for three to five years, answer the following three questions:

12. Are you married to and living with a U.S. citizen (who has been a citizen for at least three years)?

13. Have you been married to that citizen for at least three years?

14. Have you remained in the United States for at least 18 months during the past three years?

    If you answer "Yes" to all three questions—Continue reading the rest of the questions to make sure that you are eligible to apply for naturalization.

    If you answer "No" to any of the three questions—Your application will be denied.

15. Did you take a trip out of the United States for longer than six months during the past three years?

    If you answer "Yes"—Your application will be denied.

    If you answer "No"—Continue reading the rest of the questions to make sure that you are eligible to apply for naturalization.

16. Have you lived in the district or state where you are applying for naturalization for the last three months?

    If you answer "Yes"—Continue reading the rest of the questions to make sure that you are eligible to apply for naturalization.

    If you answer "No"—You must wait until you have lived there for three months before applying.

17. Can you read, write, and speak basic English? Do you know the history of the United States and its form of government?

    If you answer "Yes" to both questions—Continue reading the rest of the questions to make sure that you are eligible to apply for naturalization.

    If you answer "No" to either question—Your application will be denied unless you have a disability and are filing Form N-648, Medical Certification for Disability Exceptions.

18. Do you have a serious criminal record?

If you answer "Yes"—Your application will be denied.

If you answer "No"—Continue reading the rest of the questions to make sure that you are eligible to apply for naturalization.

19. If you are male, are you registered with the Selective Service?

If you answer "Yes"—Continue reading the rest of the questions to make sure that you are eligible to apply for naturalization.

If you answer "No"—Unless you did not enter the United States before the age of 26, or entered between the ages of 18 and 26 and did not register but have a letter from the Selective Service explaining why, you must be registered or your application will be denied. If you meet these exceptions, continue reading the questions.

20. Have you deserted from the U.S. military?

If you answer "Yes"—Your application will be denied.

If you answer "No"—Continue reading the rest of the questions to make sure that you are eligible to apply for naturalization.

21. Have you received an exemption or discharge from the U.S. military because you are an alien?

If you answer "Yes"—Your application will be denied.

If you answer "No"—Continue reading the rest of the questions to make sure that you are eligible to apply for naturalization.

22. Are you willing to serve in the military or civilian service for the United States if the law requires you to do so?

If you answer "Yes"—Continue reading the rest of the questions to make sure that you are eligible to apply for naturalization.

If you answer "No"—Unless your religious beliefs or teaching prohibit it, you must be willing to serve or your application will be denied.

23. Will you support the U.S. Constitution?

If you answer "Yes"—Continue reading the rest of the questions to make sure that you are eligible to apply for naturalization.

If you answer "No"—Your application will be denied.

24. Do you understand the oath of allegiance to the United States (see page 41), and are you willing to take it?

If you answer "Yes"—Read the rest of the questions to make sure that you are eligible to apply for naturalization.

If you answer "No"—Your application will be denied.

NOTES

_____

_____

_____

_____

_____

_____

_____

_____

_____

_____

_____

_____

_____

_____

_____

_____

_____

_____

_____

_____

_____

_____

_____

_____

_____

_____

_____

_____

_____

_____

_____

_____

_____

_____

_____

_____

_____

_____

_____

_____

_____

_____

_____

_____

_____

_____

_____

_____

_____

_____

_____

_____

_____

_____

_____

_____

_____

_____

_____

_____

_____

_____

_____

_____

_____

_____

_____

_____

_____

_____

_____

_____

_____

_____

_____

_____

_____

_____

_____

_____

_____

_____

Step 3: **Practicing Reading, Writing, and Speaking English**

To be eligible for citizenship, you must be able to read, write, and speak simple words and phrases in English. This step explains how to improve your English skills and it provides practice exercises similar to those on your test and interview.

HOW YOUR ENGLISH IS TESTED

There are three ways that your English skills are tested: reading, writing, and speaking. To see how well you read English, you are asked to read out loud. You are given one of three things to read: parts of the N-400, civics questions (which you also answer), or a number of simple sentences.

To test your writing, you are asked to write one or two simple sentences. To test your speaking ability, during your interview you are asked questions about yourself and your application.

FIVE WAYS TO IMPROVE YOUR ENGLISH SKILLS

The following five things will help improve your English skills:

1. Reading the newspaper

2. Writing your personal history

3. Reading out loud

4. Listening

5. Talking with people

Reading the Newspaper

Improving your English skills means not only practicing what you already know, but also learning more. A great way to learn new words and better understand grammar is to read the newspaper every day.

Choose a national newspaper rather than a smaller local one. Then, spend at least 20 minutes reading. As you read, write down the words you do not know. When you are finished, look up the words in a dictionary, and write the definition next to the word. Pick three of the words and write them on smaller pieces of paper or cards that you can carry with you. Check the cards a few times a day, and try using the words in a conversation.

For more practice, choose the story that had the most words you did not know in it, and read it out loud.

Writing Your Personal History

Form N-400 asks many questions about your life and experiences, and during your interview, you may be asked questions about the information you wrote on that form. This exercise helps you with the form and the interview, and it improves your English skills, too.

Tell your story, in English, by writing or typing it. Imagine someone has asked you about your life: Where are you from? What was it like there? Who are your family members? What are some happy memories? Have you traveled to other countries? Why do you want to become a U.S. citizen? Include your family history, children, and a description of the jobs you have held. Try to write a page or more about your life.

Reading Out Loud

Reading out loud, whether to yourself or another person, improves your confidence with spoken English. Try to read at least two stories or articles in front of a mirror for about 15 minutes each day. They could be stories from the newspaper, magazine articles, or pages from a book.

If you can record your voice while you are reading, you can play the recording back to hear how you are improving. The more you practice, the better you get at reading out loud.

Listening

Understanding spoken English is harder for some people than writing or reading. Conversations in stores and on the street can be difficult—people may talk quickly, have an accent that is hard to figure out, or use words you don't understand. The best way to improve your listening skills is to practice in a quiet place where there are no distractions. When you listen to the television, radio, or a book on tape (borrow these from a library), you can concentrate on what is being said. Some televisions even have "closed captioning," meaning they can print out what is being said at the bottom of the screen. Reading these captions while you listen can help you make sure you understand the conversation.

Talking with People

Talking with people is another great way to improve your English skills, but you need good listening skills at the same time. If the people you are talking with are hard to understand, stop them and let them know. They can slow down, or use different words to say the same thing. Talking with people forces you to use English instead of just studying it. Many people find that talking not only improves their English skills, but also helps them to understand better what other people are saying.

PRACTICE EXERCISES

Follow the instructions to complete the exercises, which were written to help you improve and study your English skills.

Important Terms to Define

These words are all found on Form N-400, the Application for Naturalization. Your interviewer may ask you questions about them to see if you understand the application. If you know the word, simply write its definition in the space provided. If you are not sure of a word's meaning, look it up in the dictionary or in this book and then copy the definition in the space provided.

1. allegiance _____

_____

_____

2. Constitution _____

_____

_____

3. citizen _____

_____

_____

4. Form N-400 _____

_____

_____

5. U.S. Citizenship and Immigration Services (USCIS) _____

_____

_____

6. interview _____

_____

_____

7. immigrant _____

_____

_____

8. continuous residence _____

_____

_____

9. moral character _____

_____

_____

10. naturalization _____

_____

_____

11. naturalization oath ceremony _____

_____

_____

12. fingerprint _____

_____

_____

13. oath _____

_____

_____

14. passport _____

_____

_____

15. permanent resident _____

_____

_____

Short-Answer Questions

These are the kinds of questions you may be asked during your interview. Find the answers to questions about the naturalization process in Steps 1 and 2, and answers to questions about history and government in Step 4. If you cannot answer one or more of the questions, look up the answers in this book, and test yourself again when you have completed Step 6.

1. What is one benefit of citizenship? _____

_____

_____

2. What form is used to apply for naturalization? _____

_____

_____

3. Who signs bills into laws? _____

_____

_____

4. How long is a senator's term? _____

_____

_____

5. What is the elected leader of a city called? _____

_____

_____

6. What is the preamble? _____

_____

_____

7. What is a responsibility of citizenship? _____

_____

_____

8. Who fought the Civil War? _____

_____

_____

9. What was the Emancipation Proclamation? _____

_____

_____

10. What can you do if your application for naturalization is denied? _____

_____

_____

_____

Reading Comprehension

These questions help you practice reading and writing in English. Read each passage and answer the questions that follow. All of the answers may be found in the passages.

Passage 1:

The United States government is made up of three branches. These branches are described in the Constitution. The first is the executive branch, which includes the president, the vice president, and the cabinet. The executive branch signs bills into law, commands the United States military, and negotiates with leaders from other countries. The legislative branch is led by the House of Representatives and the Senate, which together are called Congress. Congress makes laws and has the power to declare war. The judicial branch is led by the Supreme Court, and includes the entire court system of the United States. The nine justices on the Supreme Court are appointed by the president for lifetime terms. They interpret the Constitution, and their decisions cannot be overturned by any other court.

1. Who appoints Supreme Court justices? _____

    _____

    _____

2. What two bodies make up Congress? _____

    _____

3. The president's cabinet is in which branch? _____

_____

_____

4. Who has the power to declare war? _____

_____

_____

5. How long is the term of a Supreme Court justice? _____

_____

_____

Passage 2:

America is known as a melting pot because it is made up of citizens who came from many countries to have a better life. Immigrants left their countries because of different reasons. Some came to America because they needed to find work, and others came to escape from war. For many years, immigrants came to America by passing the Statue of Liberty, which was a gift of friendship from France, and landing on Ellis Island in the New York Harbor. Twelve million immigrants passed through Ellis Island from 1892 until it closed in 1954.

6. Where is Ellis Island? _____

_____

_____

7. How many immigrants passed through Ellis Island? _____

_____

_____

8. Immigrants come to America for many reasons—name one. _____

_____

_____

9. Where did the Statue of Liberty come from? _____

_____

_____

10. Why is America called a melting pot? _____

_____

_____

Reading Out Loud

During your citizenship test you must read 10 sentences out loud. The sentences are very similar to the following ones. Practice reading them out loud to yourself, a family member, or a friend.

1. I live in America.

2. Every citizen should vote.

3. The boy runs fast.

4. She wants to find a job.

5. I have two children.

6. His car is blue.

7. Today it is raining.

8. I shop at the grocery store.

9. There is a big tree in my yard.

10. The children watch television.

ANSWERS AND EXPLANATIONS

Here are the answers and explanations for the practice questions. For more practice, see the practice test in Step 6 and the 100 Frequently Asked U.S History and Government Questions and Answers at the end of this book.

Important Terms to Define

1. Allegiance is loyalty to a nation. When you say the Pledge of Allegiance, you promise to be loyal to the United States.

2. The Constitution is the supreme law of the land. It explains our laws, our government, and the powers of the government.

3. A citizen is someone who by birth or naturalization owes loyalty to a country and is protected by it.

4. Form N-400 is the Application for Naturalization.

5. The USCIS is the government agency that helps immigrants become citizens.

6. After you file Form N-400, you get an appointment for an interview. In the interview, you meet with someone from the USCIS to go over your application and take the English and Civics tests.

7. An immigrant is someone who leaves one country to live in another.

8. Continuous residence refers to the length of time a permanent resident lives in the United States without taking a long trip out of the country. Most people who apply for naturalization need five years of continuous residence.

9. Moral character refers to the kind of person you are. To be eligible for citizenship, you must be of good moral character. If you committed a certain type of crime, you may not be eligible to become a citizen.

10. Naturalization is the way an immigrant becomes a citizen of the United States.

11. During the naturalization oath ceremony you take the oath of allegiance and become a U.S. citizen.

12. A fingerprint is an impression of your fingertip. Fingerprints are taken after you file the Application for Naturalization. They are used for identification because no two people's fingerprints are alike.

13. An oath is a promise. When you say the oath of allegiance to the United States, you promise to renounce foreign allegiances, support the Constitution, and serve the United States.

14. A passport is a government document that proves citizenship and allows you to travel to other countries.

15. A permanent resident is someone who has permanent resident status according to immigration law. He or she has a permanent resident card. After five years, a permanent resident can apply for naturalization.

Short-Answer Questions

After each answer, the step in which the answer may be found is given.

1. Benefits of citizenship include the right to vote, having a U.S. passport, and having government protection when traveling outside the U.S. (Step 2)

2. To apply for naturalization, you use Form N-400. (Step 2)

3. The president signs bills into laws. (Step 4)

4. Senators are elected to six-year terms. (Step 4)

5. The elected leader of a city is a mayor. (Step 4)

6. The preamble is the introduction to the Constitution. (Step 4)

7. The responsibilities of citizenship include giving up allegiance to other countries, supporting and defending the U.S. Constitution, swearing allegiance to the United States, serving the United States, registering to vote and voting, serving on a jury if called, and tolerating the differences of other citizens. (Step 2)

8. The Civil War was fought by Northern free states (the Union) against Southern slave-holding states (the Confederacy). (Step 4)

9. The Emancipation Proclamation was an order issued by President Lincoln to free slaves in the 11 confederate states. (Step 4)

10. If your application for naturalization is denied, you can request a hearing. (Step 2)

Reading Comprehension

1. The president appoints Supreme Court justices.

2. Congress is made up of the House of Representatives and the Senate.

3. The president's cabinet is part of the executive branch.

4. Congress has the power to declare war.

5. Supreme Court justices serve lifetime terms.

6. Ellis Island is in New York Harbor.

7. Twelve million immigrants passed through Ellis Island.

8. Immigrants came to America to find work; they also came to escape war.

9. The Statue of Liberty came from France.

10. America is called a melting pot because it is made up of people from many different countries.

NOTES

_____

_____

_____

_____

_____

_____

_____

_____

_____

_____

_____

_____

_____

_____

_____

_____

_____

_____

_____

_____

_____

_____

_____

_____

_____

_____

Step 4: Learning about U.S. History and Government

During your interview with the USCIS, your knowledge of U.S. history is tested, along with your knowledge about how the government works. This portion of the interview is known as the civics test. The interviewer asks you to answer a set of questions on history and government out loud, or to take a written multiple-choice test. The test includes up to 20 questions.

In this part of Step 4, you learn everything you need to know about history to pass that test. Later on in the step, you review the basics of government.

THE COLONIAL PERIOD

During the colonial period, settlers from Europe came to America and formed a new country.

Important Terms and Names

Native Americans	Revolutionary War
Pilgrims	Declaration of Independence
Jamestown	George Washington
Mayflower	Thomas Jefferson
slavery	13 colonies

Native Population

Before Europeans came to what is now called North America, millions of Native Americans lived in the so-called "New World." Although it is not known how many distinct tribes or nations of Native Americans were here, early European settlers said they met approximately 60 tribes just in the land east of the Mississippi River. These tribes had their own languages, styles of clothing and shelter, and methods of hunting, growing, and preparing food. Because of these differences, and the fact that the tribes were geographically separated from one another, it was impossible for these native people to join together and successfully negotiate with and protect themselves from the Europeans who began exploring North America in the 1400s.

European Explorers

During the 1400s and 1500s, many of the kings and queens of Europe sent men across the oceans to find gold and claim land. Explorers from Spain, England, and France came to North America during this time. The Spanish claimed much of the land, and its riches, that stretched from what is now California, south to Argentina, and east to Florida. The French took parts of Canada and upper northeastern North America. The English claimed much of the East Coast.

The Colonists

King James II of England sent ships full of settlers to the New World. The Virginia Company established Jamestown (named for the king), the first successful English settlement. John Smith led Jamestown, and developed it for one reason: to make money to send back to the Virginia Company in England. However, the settlers had a difficult time in the New World. They were under constant attack from the Algonquin Indians, many starved during the winter, and the fort they managed to build burned. Thousands of settlers lost their lives. After 14 years, the king made Jamestown a colony, taking control from the Virginia Company.

In 1620, over 100 Pilgrims sailed on the Mayflower from England to Plymouth, where they established the Massachusetts Bay Colony. The Pilgrims were Protestants who had not been allowed to practice their religion freely in England. When they landed in Plymouth, they agreed to form a government and to abide by its laws. Their agreement, signed by the 41 men aboard the ship, was called the Mayflower Compact.

When the Pilgrims settled in Plymouth, they received help from the Native Americans, who taught them how to find and raise food. The Pilgrims thanked them after their first successful harvest by inviting their Native American friends to a feast, known as the first Thanksgiving.

13 Colonies

Over the next hundred years, 12 other colonies grew along the East Coast from New Hampshire to Georgia. Pilgrims who moved away from the Massachusetts Bay Colony established some of these colonies and new settlers founded others. The New England colonies (Connecticut, Rhode Island, Massachusetts, and New Hampshire) had small farms but excelled in shipbuilding, fishing, trading, and producing rum. The middle colonies (New York, New Jersey, Pennsylvania, and Delaware) produced wheat on larger farms and had large port cities like New York and Philadelphia. The southern colonies (Maryland, Virginia, North Carolina, South Carolina, and Georgia) grew tobacco on large plantations and corn and rice on smaller farms.

THE RISE OF SLAVERY

In 1619, the first Africans arrived in Jamestown. By 1660, there were hundreds of thousands of Africans in America, most in the southern colonies. They worked on farms and plantations, and many of them were allowed to buy their freedom after seven years of work. However, in 1660, Virginia passed laws that made black servants and their children lifelong slaves. The other southern slave-holding states passed similar laws, making slaves the property of their owners. They could be bought and sold, and had no legal status or rights. By the start of the American Revolution a hundred years later, there were about 4 million slaves in the United States.

Anger toward England

Although the colonists first came to America looking for freedom, England kept firm control over them. The colonists were not allowed to rule themselves, and had to pay many taxes to the king. The English collected tax money from the colonists for paper, sugar, tea, and many other items. The stamp tax, for example, had to be paid for every printed piece of paper used by the colonists. The colonists reacted by joining together to fight the taxes. Many stopped buying English products, including a shipment of tea that arrived in the Boston harbor. The colonists boarded the ship and dumped the tea into the water in what was known as the Boston Tea Party. England responded by closing the harbor and passing even more laws to control the colonists.

In 1774, representatives from 12 of the 13 colonies traveled to Philadelphia to organize a protest against England. They called themselves the Continental Congress, and came up with a list of demands, including stopping the collection of many taxes. They agreed that if England did not meet those demands, they would meet again the next year.

The Revolutionary War Breaks Out

Of all the colonists, those from Massachusetts were treated the worst by England. As a result, they began to collect weapons and organize a group of soldiers known as Minutemen. When the Minutemen found out that British soldiers were coming to arrest them and take their weapons, they fought back.

The Revolutionary War began with the "shot heard 'round the world," fired by the Minutemen at the soldiers. Word spread throughout the colonies, and many more colonists joined the fight. In Virginia, Patrick Henry inspired his colony to go to war with a famous speech in which he declared, "Give me liberty or give me death." George Washington was named General of the growing Continental Army. As the fighting continued, the Continental Congress met again, and decided that they wanted independence from England.

The Declaration of Independence

Five members of the Continental Congress, led by Thomas Jefferson, wrote a document explaining to England that the colonies wanted their independence. It was adopted on July 4, 1776, and was called the Declaration of Independence. In it, Jefferson explained that it was within the colonists' rights to be independent, and listed the things that England did to make them want to form their own government. Jefferson stated that "all men are created equal," and they have the right to "life, liberty, and the pursuit of happiness."

However, the colonists' declaration alone did not give them independence. The Continental Army still needed to win the war against England. The French army came to the aid of the Continental Army, which was led by General George Washington, and the Revolutionary War was finally won in 1781.

THE FLAG OF THE UNITED STATES

The Continental Congress passed the first Flag Act in 1777, which said that the U.S. flag would be made of 13 alternating red and white stripes, with 13 white stars on a blue background. The number 13 represented the original 13 states (see Figure 4.1). As new states became part of the country, stars were added for each, and the stars were eventually placed in rows. Although there are now 50 stars, representing the 50 states, there are still 13 stripes representing the original 13 states (see Figure 4.2).

Figure 4.1   The First U.S. Flag

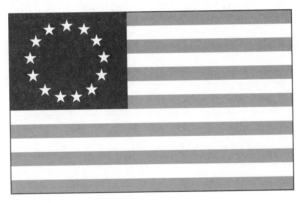

Figure 4.2   The Current U.S. Flag

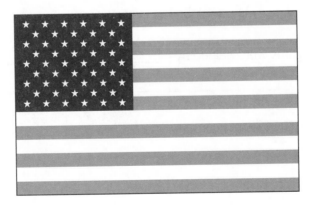

Practice Questions

1. From what country did the colonists become independent? _____

_____

_____

2. Where was the first successful English colony in North America settled?

_____

_____

3. Slaves were owned for life and had no legal _____.

4. Who led the army to victory over the English in the Revolutionary War?

_____

_____

5. The main writer of the Declaration of Independence was

_____.

6. How many original colonies were there? _____

7. Independence Day is celebrated every year on _____.

8. The Pilgrims were helped by _____

_____.

9. Why did the Pilgrims come to America? _____

_____

_____

10. The 13 stripes on the flag represent _____

_____.

Answers and Explanations

1. The colonists gained their independence from England by winning the Revolutionary War.

   Explanation: The American colonies were under British rule from the time they were first settled. After over 100 years, the colonists wanted to govern themselves and to stop paying taxes to a king they believed was not being fair to them.

2. The first successful English colony in North America was settled in Jamestown, Virginia.

   Explanation: The colony was first run by the Virginia Company, but after 14 years the king took control.

3. Slaves were owned for life and had no legal rights.

4. General George Washington led the Continental Army to victory in the Revolutionary War.

   Explanation: Washington led the army to victory by coordinating the French, Spanish, and Dutch troops with his own. The English surrendered after the battle at Yorktown, which Washington planned and led.

5. Thomas Jefferson was the main author of the Declaration of Independence.

6. There were 13 original colonies: Connecticut, Delaware, Georgia, Maryland, Massachusetts, New Hampshire, New Jersey, New York, North Carolina, Rhode Island, Pennsylvania, South Carolina, and Virginia.

   Explanation: The first settlements were established in Plymouth and Jamestown. Over many years, the settlements grew into colonies, and some people left to start new colonies. By the mid-1700s, there were 13 English colonies along the east coast of what is now the United States.

7. Independence Day is celebrated every year on July 4.

8. The Pilgrims were helped by Native Americans.

9. The Pilgrims came to America to have the freedom to practice their religion as they wished.

   Explanation: In England, many people, including the Pilgrims, were persecuted for practicing their religion.

10. The 13 stripes represent the original 13 colonies.

FROM THE U.S. CONSTITUTION TO THE CIVIL WAR

The writing of the Constitution and beginning years of independence were not easy. America fought two wars during this time, and had to deal with the difficult issue of slavery.

Important Terms and Names

Constitution

supreme law of the land

George Washington

Louisiana Purchase

War of 1812

"The Star-Spangled Banner"

Free and slave states

Underground Railroad

Confederate States of America

Abraham Lincoln

The Constitution

Once the United States of America was established, leaders from each state met to decide on laws and a form of government. They began writing the Constitution, which became the supreme law of the land in 1789, almost 13 years after the Declaration of Independence was ratified. The Constitution established the court system, the Congress, and the presidency, including an explanation of how to select the president and the qualifications needed for the position.

Soon after the Constitution became law, George Washington was elected as president of the United States, which also meant he was the first commander in chief of the U.S. military. Because he was the first president, Washington had to decide how to use the power of his office. He set up the first cabinet, or group of advisors, toured different areas of the country, and helped establish the country's financial system.

Washington's success as the first president resulted in his nickname, "father of our country." He was president for nine years, followed by John Adams, who served four years. Thomas Jefferson was elected the third president in 1801.

Figure 4.3   The Louisiana Purchase

Westward Expansion

A year into Jefferson's presidency, he negotiated a deal with Napoleon Bonaparte of France to buy the Louisiana Territory. Known as the Louisiana Purchase, this deal doubled the size of the United States (see Figure 4.3).

Jefferson chose two men, Meriwether Lewis and William Clark, to explore the new land. Lewis and Clark traveled from St. Louis, Missouri, to the Pacific coast of Oregon, keeping notes about the landscape, Native Americans, plants, and animals they encountered. They established a route that would be followed by countless others as settlers moved west. In order to encourage people to leave the Eastern states for the new territory, government land was sold very cheaply to those who in return promised to work that land.

War of 1812

Thirty years after granting independence to the United States, England was still trying to control the new country. It captured over 10,000 American sailors on oceans around the world, and provided weapons to Native Americans in the west so they could fight against settlers. England also had a large army in Canada.

In 1812, President Madison declared the Second War of Independence, now known as the War of 1812. British troops invaded the United States, took over many forts, burned Washington DC, and attempted to take Baltimore Harbor. The war ended in 1814, after the Americans won the Battle of New Orleans and both countries signed a peace treaty.

THE NATIONAL ANTHEM

In 1814, Francis Scott Key visited the British fleet in Chesapeake Bay, Virginia, to ask them to release a prison taken after the burning of Washington DC. Key was held on a ship overnight as the British tried to take Fort McHenry. When he woke the next day, he saw the American flag still flying over the fort. His happiness inspired him to write a poem about the event. The poem was set to music, and "The Star-Spangled Banner" became the official national anthem in 1931.

Slavery Grows

Although Congress stopped the slave trade in 1808; Southern states were allowed to keep the slaves they already owned. Southern farmers grew cotton, sugar, and tobacco—all crops that were in great demand and that needed much labor to get from the field to the market. They had to be picked carefully by hand, which took time.

As America added new areas in the South and West, Southern farmers were able to farm even more land, and slave labor was used. They made huge profits because they did not have to pay their workers.

However, in the Northern states—known as Free States—owning slaves was against the law. As new states were added to the Union, Northerners wanted them to be free, and Southerners argued that they should be slave states. Some Northerners began speaking out against slavery, and formed the Underground Railroad to help slaves escape to freedom. This escape route was made up of individuals who guided slaves from one safe place to another until they reached a Free State. Tens of thousands of slaves gained their freedom through the Underground Railroad. However, the number of slaves doubled during this time, growing from 2 to 4 million by 1860.

The Civil War

In 1861, Abraham Lincoln became president. He was against slavery. The Southern slave-holding states worried that he would make slavery illegal, and so seven of them declared that they were no longer part of the United States.

A month after Lincoln took office, Southerners shot at federal troops in South Carolina, and the Civil War began. Four more states declared that they were leaving the Union, and 11 Southern states formed the Confederate States of America. They elected Jefferson Davis as theiri president.

The Civil War was the bloodiest war in American history. In a battle at Antietam Creek in Maryland, 4,000 soldiers were killed in one day. In Gettysburg, Pennsylvania, a three-day battle left over 27,000 dead, wounded, or missing. General Robert E. Lee led the Confederate army, and General Ulysses Grant was the leader of the Northern, or Union, army.

During the war, President Lincoln issued the Emancipation Proclamation, which freed all slaves in the 11 confederate states. It also allowed African Americans to join the Union army. After four years, the Civil War ended with General Lee's surrender, which brought the Confederate states back into the Union. Lincoln only enjoyed the victory for a short time—he was assassinated while sitting in a theater by Confederate John Wilkes Booth one week after the war ended.

Practice Questions

1. The supreme law of the land is the _____.

2. What is the national anthem of the United States? _____

   _____

   _____

3. The Southern general whose surrender ended the Civil War was

   _____.

4. The War of 1812 was also called the Second War of Independence because
   the United States fought which country in it?

   _____

   _____

5. President Jefferson bought land from France in a deal called the _____

   _____

   _____.

6. Why is George Washington called the father of our country?

   _____

   _____

   _____

7. The president who freed the slaves was _____

   _____.

8. The Southern states that left the Union became known as _____

_____

_____

9. When was the Constitution written? _____

_____

10. What did the Emancipation Proclamation do? _____

_____

_____

_____

Answers and Explanations

1. The supreme law of the land is the Constitution.

2. The national anthem is "The Star-Spangled Banner."

   Explanation: Written during the war of 1812 by Francis Scott Key, "The Star Spangled Banner" is a patriotic song about the American flag and America's victory over and freedom from its enemies.

3. The Southern general whose surrender ended the Civil War was Robert E. Lee.

4. The United States fought England in the War of 1812, which is the same country they fought in the Revolutionary War.

   Explanation: Although it declared independence almost 40 years earlier, the United States still had problems with England. England tried to control the new country, and America fought back in what has been called the Second War of Independence.

5. President Jefferson bought from France the Louisiana Territory. (This is known as the Louisiana Purchase.)

6. George Washington is known as the father of our country because he was the first president.

   Explanation: As the first president, Washington had to set the example for future presidents, deciding how to use the power of the office. He paved the way for future presidents, leading many to call him the father of our country.

7. Abraham Lincoln freed the slaves.

8. The Southern states that left the Union became known as the Confederate States of America.

9. The Constitution was written in 1787.

   Explanation: The United States of America was officially an independent country, but until the Constitution was written, its form of government and system of laws were not determined. The Constitution did not become supreme law of the land until 1789, when all states agreed to it.

10. The Emancipation Proclamation freed the slaves.

    Explanation: Issued by Abraham Lincoln during the Civil War, the Emancipation Proclamation made it illegal to own slaves in the states that had left the Union to form the Confederate States of America.

FROM RECONSTRUCTION TO WORLD WAR I

After the Civil War, America grew as people from many countries came to make better lives for themselves and their families. At the beginning of the twentieth century, the nation came together to fight in World War I.

Important Terms and Names

Reconstruction

Andrew Johnson

Civil Rights Amendment

immigration

melting pot

Ellis Island

World War I

Allies

President Wilson

League of Nations

Reconstruction

After Lincoln's death, following the rules of the Constitution, his vice president, Andrew Johnson, became president. Johnson had to bring the country together again, or "reconstruct" it, after the Civil War. During Reconstruction, the Confederate states came back to the Union, and the Constitution was changed to make slavery illegal. In response, most of the Southern states passed laws that made it very difficult for slaves to be free. The Congress passed the Fourteenth Amendment, known as the Civil Rights Amendment, and the Fifteenth Amendment to give African Americans full citizenship and the right to vote.

Nonetheless, laws did not change the way Southerners felt and acted; most simply ignored the new laws, while others became angry and violent toward freed slaves. They were also angry with the president and Congress, who they believed were forcing a new way of life on them. Life for African Americans in the South was in many ways as bad as it was when they were slaves.

Immigration

The United States is often referred to as a "melting pot," a place where people from many other countries, for many reasons, come to live. These people bring with them their cultures, languages, and customs, and come together to form one nation. The original colonies were settled by English immigrants seeking religious freedom. By the time they founded the United States, other English immigrants, such as the Quakers, and thousands from Germany and Ireland had joined them, along with hundreds of thousands of Africans brought to America by force in the slave trade.

Because of famines in Ireland, millions of Irish immigrants arrived in the 1800s. Poverty and the wish to practice their religion freely brought millions of Swedes and Norwegians here at the same time. Persecution was the reason about 2 million European Jews came to America beginning in 1880, and poverty caused the same number of Italians to seek a better life in America.

ELLIS ISLAND

Immigrants from Europe came on ships that landed in the New York harbor. During the late 1800s and early 1900s, there were so many people arriving each day that an immigration station was opened on Ellis Island to handle them. To get to Ellis Island, the ships had to pass the Statue of Liberty, which became a symbol of welcome to the country (see Figure 4.4). During the 62 years it was open, 12 million immigrants landed on Ellis Island before they were allowed to enter America.

Figure 4.4   The Statue of Liberty

World War I

In 1914, war broke out in Europe. The United States, under President Woodrow Wilson, tried to get England and Germany to agree to a peace treaty after three years of fighting, but was not successful. America stayed neutral, taking neither side, until German submarines destroyed American ships in the Atlantic Ocean. President Wilson declared war against Germany in 1917. The United States joined the Allies (countries who were already fighting Germany together), which included England, France, Russia, and Italy. The war ended in 1918 when a peace treaty was signed in Paris.

When the treaty was signed, President Wilson suggested that all of the countries that had been in the war form the League of Nations, a group that would help countries settle their differences so they could prevent another World War.

Practice Questions

1. The period after the Civil War, when the Confederate States came back into the Union, is known as _____.

2. List three of the reasons why people immigrated to the United States.

   _____

   _____

   _____

3. The statue in New York that welcomed immigrants is called

   _____.

4. Alongside which countries did America fight during World War I?

   _____

5. The first immigration station that millions of immigrants arrived at was

   _____.

6. When Lincoln died, his _____,

   Andrew Johnson, became president.

7. In World War I, who was America's enemy? _____

   _____

8. During Reconstruction, the Constitution was changed to make _____

   _____ illegal.

9. Which president had the idea for the League of Nations?

_____

10. Because it is made up of people from many different cultures and countries, the United States is sometimes called a

_____.

Answers and Explanations

1. The period after the Civil War, when the Confederate states came back into the Union, was called Reconstruction.

2. Some of the reasons people immigrated to the United States included seeking religious freedom and escaping from famines, wars, persecution, and poverty.

   Explanation: Most Americans are the descendants of immigrants, who came to this country because they believed they would have a better life here.

3. The Statue of Liberty welcomed immigrants in New York.

4. The Americans joined the allies France, Russia, England, and Italy, in World War I.

   Explanation: Because Germany's attack on American ships brought the United States into the war, the United States joined the group of allies that was fighting Germany.

5. Millions of immigrants landed on Ellis Island before they were allowed into America.

   Explanation: Because so many immigrants were arriving daily in the late 1800s, an immigration station was built where they could be processed. On Ellis Island, the immigrants were checked to make sure they had no legal or medical problems before they were allowed into the country.

6. After Lincoln died, Vice President Andrew Johnson became president.

7. Germany was America's enemy during World War I.

   Explanation: The United States did not want to get involved in the war in Europe, and had no reason to do so until German submarines began attacking American ships in the Atlantic Ocean. Congress declared war on Germany in 1917.

8. The Constitution was changed to make slavery illegal during Reconstruction.

9. Woodrow Wilson first came up with the idea for the League of Nations.

   Explanation: After the First World War, President Wilson wanted to ensure that the world would never be at war again. He proposed that all of the countries that had been involved in the war form a group called the League of Nations that would work to negotiate and settle differences between its members.

10. A "melting pot" refers to a place that is made up of people from different cultures and backgrounds.

FROM THE AFTERMATH OF WORLD WAR I TO THE PRESENT

During the twentieth century, America continued to change. People demanded equal rights for all, no matter whether they were male or female, black or white. The Great Depression created widespread poverty, but also sparked important changes in the government. The United States was also involved in conflicts with other nations, including World War II and the Cold War.

Important Terms and Names

Great Depression	Pearl Harbor
Franklin Roosevelt	segregation
New Deal	John F. Kennedy
Nineteenth Amendment	Dr. Martin Luther King Jr.
World War II	Ronald Reagan

Great Depression

In 1929, the stock market "crashed," meaning that its value dropped very quickly. Businesses, factories, and banks closed, leaving many people without work or savings. By 1932, one out of every four Americans was jobless, and poverty was widespread.

In 1933, Franklin Roosevelt became president, and promised to bring America out of the Depression. He introduced many government programs, together called the New Deal, which would help the country to recover. The New Deal created jobs, helped banks and businesses reopen, and started Social Security.

WOMEN'S RIGHTS

African Americans were not the only group in the United States fighting for their rights. Women were not allowed to vote in most states until 1920, when the Nineteenth Amendment, which gave them that right, was added to the Constitution. The amendment was a victory for the thousands of American women who were a part of the suffrage movement, working to make sure that all citizens—men and women—were given the right to vote.

World War II

In 1939, war broke out in Europe when Germany took Poland, invaded France, and began bombing England. Under Adolf Hitler, the German army attacked other countries all over Europe, and moved into Russia and Africa.

The United States did not want to get involved in another war, and initially stayed out of the conflict. However, in 1941, the Japanese bombed the U.S. Navy base in Pearl Harbor, Hawaii, destroying five ships and 180 planes, and killing over 2,300 Americans. Congress declared war on Japan the next day. Japan's allies Germany and Italy declared war on the United States a few days later.

World War II was fought in Europe and in the Pacific, where Japan was invading China, Singapore, and other countries. The United States had armies in both places, and was an ally of England, France, and Russia. After four years of fighting, Italy surrendered in 1943; Germany surrendered two years later. World War II did not end until later in 1945, when Japan surrendered after the United States dropped atomic bombs on two of its cities.

After the war, the countries that had fought in it realized that the League of Nations, which was formed after World War I, did not fulfill its purpose of preventing another conflict. A new organization was proposed to take its place and do a better job of keeping peace. It was called the United Nations, a term used a few years earlier by President Roosevelt to describe the allies who were fighting in World War II. Fifty-one countries were members of the United Nations when it was created in 1945.

The Cold War

After World War II, Russia took over many neighboring countries and incorporated them into the Soviet Union. The line between most of Europe and the Soviet Union was called the Iron Curtain. President Truman and England's Prime Minister Winston Churchill worked together to try to keep the Soviet Union from threatening any other countries. The United States and the Soviet Union began making nuclear weapons, weapons much more powerful than the atomic bombs of World War II. They were in an "arms race" to see who could have the most, and most powerful weapons. The Cold War got its name from the fact that because the weapons were so powerful, both countries were afraid to use them, and therefore never fought each other directly.

BECOMING A NATION OF 50 STATES ————————————

In January of 1959, Alaska became the 49th state. A few months later, Hawaii was admitted as the 50th (and last) state, and the number of stars on the flag was increased to match the new number of states.

The Civil Rights Movement

At the time that the United States became independent, African Americans did not have the same rights as white Americans. After almost 200 years, although the laws of the country said they were equal, African Americans were not treated fairly. Blacks in the South were not allowed to vote, and were not allowed to go to the same schools as whites. Many public places, such as swimming pools and movie theaters, did not allow blacks. This practice of separating the races was known as segregation.

After World War II people around the country began speaking out against segregation and other types of inequality. They joined together as a movement in 1955, when a strong leader emerged. Dr. Martin Luther King Jr. attracted many people, black and white, to work for equality for African Americans. By 1963, under Dr. King's leadership, over 1,000 demonstrations and protests were held across the South; President Kennedy sent a new civil rights bill to Congress; and in August over 200,000 people attended the March on Washington. The march was the largest political protest in U.S. history at that time. Congress passed Kennedy's bill the following year, six months after Kennedy was assassinated.

Like the laws passed 100 years earlier that freed slaves and gave them limited rights, the Civil Rights Act did not change the way people thought and behaved. Black churches were bombed, and many protesters were injured, jailed, or murdered. Martin Luther King continued to lead peaceful protests until 1968, when he was assassinated, days before Congress passed another civil rights bill.

The End of the Cold War

During the 1970s and 1980s, the Cold War continued as the two world superpowers—the Soviet Union and United States—remained enemies. During that time, many of the countries that made up the Soviet Union wanted to be democratic, and fought against the Soviet Union for their freedom. The United States supported many of those countries with money and weapons. In 1985, the Soviet Union's new leader, Mikhail Gorbachev, realized the need for a better relationship with America. He met with President Reagan, and the two superpowers signed the INF Treaty, promising to destroy many nuclear weapons.

By 1990, the Soviet Union was falling apart. Many of its republics (countries that had been taken over by the Soviet Union and made Communist) declared their independence. Months before the government voted to end the Soviet Union, Gorbachev met with President George H. W. Bush and the two signed a second treaty, agreeing to limit their numbers of nuclear weapons even more.

In 1991, the Soviet Union was divided into four independent countries: Belarus, Kazakhstan, Russia, and Ukraine. Russia was no longer a superpower; it had an improved relationship with the United States, and the two countries agreed to reduce their numbers of weapons. The Cold War was over.

Practice Questions

1. American women were not allowed to vote in most states until _____.

2. Why did the United States enter World War II? _____

_____

_____

3. The Cold War ended in 1991, when _____
   was divided into four independent countries.

4. Who was Dr. Martin Luther King, Jr.? _____

_____

_____

5. The United States' allies during World War II were _____
   and _____.

6. World War II ended with the United States dropped two atomic bombs on

_____.

7. Who was president of the United States when the cold war ended?

_____

8. During the Cold War, the line between the Soviet Union and the rest of Europe
   was called _____.

9. Which president helped America to recover from the Great Depression?

_____

10. What is segregation? _____

_____

_____

Answers and Explanations

1. As of the year 1920, American women were allowed to vote in most states.

2. The Japanese bombed the American naval base in Pearl Harbor, and the United States declared war on them, bringing the country into World War II.

   Explanation: Until attacked, America did not want to get involved in the war; after Japan's bombing, which killed 2,300 Americans, Congress declared war. A few days later, Germany and Italy declared war on the United States.

3. The Soviet Union was divided into four nations in 1991, when the Cold War ended.

4. Dr. Martin Luther King, Jr. was an African American who led the civil rights movement in the 1950s and 1960s.

   Explanation: Under Dr. King's leadership, protestors joined together to form the civil rights movement, which worked to end unfair treatment of African Americans. King led the movement from 1955 until he was assassinated in 1968.

5. England and France were allies of the United States during World War II.

6. The United States dropped two atomic bombs on Japan, thus ending World War II.

7. When the Cold War ended, the President of the United States was George H. W. Bush.

Explanation: George H. W. Bush, the 41st president, served one term, from 1989–1993.

8. The line between the Soviet Union and the rest of Europe was called the Iron Curtain.

9. Franklin Roosevelt helped America recover from the Great Depression.

Explanation: Roosevelt introduced many programs, which together were called the New Deal. Those programs created jobs, helped banks and businesses reopen, and started Social Security.

10. Segregation is the separation of races, such as keeping blacks from using the same swimming pools, attending the same schools, and eating at the same restaurants as whites.

Explanation: Although African Americans were equal under the law, the people did not treat them as equals. For example, the schools they could attend were not as good as schools for whites; they could not buy houses in white neighborhoods; and could not use the same swimming pools or drinking fountains as whites.

FEDERAL AND STATE POWERS

In this section, you learn the information you need to know about the U.S. government in order to pass the Civics test given during your USCIS interview.

The Constitution explains how the organization of the government, including the election process of leaders and the kinds of powers they can and cannot have. Most states use a system for their government that is similar to the one used by federal government.

Important Terms and Names

checks and balances

executive branch

legislative branch

Senate

House of Representatives

judicial branch

Supreme Court

cabinet

electoral college

governor

Three Branches of Government: "Separation of Powers"

To make sure that the United States would not be ruled by one person, or even one group, the writers of the Constitution created a government in which power was separated into three branches. This separation of power is supposed to provide checks and balances. Each branch can "check" on the others to make sure that they are working the way they are supposed to, and that no one branch has all the power—it is "balanced" among the three.

The Executive Branch

The president heads the first, or executive, branch of the government, and it includes the vice president and the members of the president's cabinet (his or her advisors). It is the president's job to execute, or carry out, federal laws and recommend new ones; command the armed forces; direct national defense and foreign policy; deal with foreign governments; and perform ceremonial duties. The president can veto, or reject, bills passed by Congress so they do not become laws. The president is elected every four years in November, and is sworn in, or inaugurated, in January of the following year. Once inaugurated, the president and his or her family move to the White House in Washington DC, where they live for the length of his or her term.

HOW IS A PRESIDENT ELECTED?

When voters go to the polls on Election Day, they're not really voting for the president. Each state has a group of "electors" who pledge to vote for the candidate who gets the most votes from the people (known as the state's popular vote). The number of electors equals the number of that state's members of Congress (two senators plus the number of representatives, which is based on population size), so some states have more electoral votes than others do. About a month after the election, the Electoral College meets to choose the president officially. Because the electors almost always vote for the candidate who won the popular vote, it is easy to figure out who will win the Electoral College votes for each state by seeing who won the popular vote in that state.

The Legislative Branch

Congress heads the second branch, or legislative branch, of the government. Two bodies make up Congress, the House of Representatives, which has 435 members, and the Senate, which has two senators from every state (100 total). The number of representatives for each state is based on population, which is why Vermont has one representative and California has over 50. States vote for their own representatives and senators. Representatives serve two-year terms, and senators serve six-year terms; there is no limit to the number of terms they may serve.

Congress's job is to make laws. Laws begin as bills, which are introduced in the House and the Senate. If a bill gets a majority of votes in both the House and Senate, it becomes a law. Congress also has the power to declare war, write spending bills (House), impeach officials (Senate), and approve presidential nominations and treaties (Senate).

The Judicial Branch

The Supreme Court heads the third, or judicial, branch, and it includes all of the courts in the United States court system. The Supreme Court is made up of nine justices who are appointed by the president, and who have no term limit. The judicial branch's powers include interpreting the Constitution, reviewing laws, and deciding cases involving states' rights. The Supreme Court is the highest court in the land, and its decisions cannot be overturned by any other court.

Branches of State and Local Governments

In addition to the federal government, states, cities, and towns have their own governments. Most states use a three-branch system that is similar to the structure of the federal government. Instead of a president, states are led by a governor, who is the head of the executive branch. Cities and towns elect a mayor to lead them.

States also have a legislative branch made up of two bodies (except for Nebraska, which has one) that go by different names. Some states call them the Senate and House of Representatives, and others have a General Assembly instead of a House of Representatives. State legislative bodies, like federal ones, have the power to make laws. In cities and towns, citizens elect people to serve on city councils. These legislative bodies also make laws.

The United States court system is made up of many courts that have different levels of authority. State courts range from the Supreme Court, which is the highest in the state, to county and city courts, which hear local cases. Higher courts can review many of the decisions made by lower courts.

Practice Questions

1. Why are there three branches of government? _____

_____

_____

_____

2. The elected leader of a state is the _____

_____.

3. Who elects the president? _____

_____

4. The _____
   branch of government makes the laws.

5. The highest court in the land is the _____

_____.

6. The _____
   is the legislative body in a city or town.

7. The president's advisors are called the _____

_____.

8. What is the Electoral College? _____

_____

_____

9. What are the three branches of government? _____

_____

_____

_____

10. A mayor is the elected leader of a _____

or _____.

Answers and Explanations

1. There are three branches of government to separate power and provide checks and balances.

   Explanation: The writers of the Constitution did not want all of the power to go to one person or one group. They believed the three branches would prevent that from happening.

2. The elected leader of a state is called the governor.

3. The Electoral College elects the president.

   Explanation: Although many believe the citizens of the United States elect their president directly, they are actually voting for the candidate they want their Electoral College members to vote for.

4. The legislative branch makes laws.

   Explanation: Bills, or ideas for future laws, are introduced in Congress. If a bill gets a majority of votes in the Senate and the House, it becomes a law.

5. The highest court in the United States is the U.S. Supreme Court.

6. City councils are the legislative bodies in cities or towns.

   Explanation: Like the legislative branches of federal and state government, city councils can make laws.

7. The president's advisors are called the cabinet.

8. The Electoral College is a group of electors from each state who choose the president.

   Explanation: Each state has the same number of electors as members of Congress, and those electors promise to choose the candidate who won the popular vote in their state. They meet about one month after the general election to elect the president.

9. The three branches of government are the executive branch, the legislative branch, and the judicial branch.

10. A mayor is the elected leader of a city or town.

INFORMATION TO RESEARCH

When taking the naturalization exam, you may be asked to name the current president, vice president, chief justice of the Supreme Court, congresspeople from your state, your state governor, and your mayor. The exam may also ask you to name your state capital. The Internet is probably the fastest and easiest way to find this information, but if you do not have Internet access, your local library can help you get these names to study.

CITIZENS' RIGHTS AND THE CONSTITUTION

As soon as the Constitution was written, it was changed. These changes, called amendments, have been made throughout the history of the United States.

Important Terms and Names

supreme law of the land	freedom of religion
amendment	freedom of the press
term limit	right to bear arms
Bill of Rights	voter
freedom of speech	Pledge of Allegiance

The U.S. Constitution and Important Principles

The United States Constitution explains the U.S. form of government and laws. It was written in 1787 by leaders from each state. Because these leaders had once been ruled by a country with one all-powerful leader (the king) they knew the kinds of problems created by that form of government, and they wanted something different.

There are three parts to the Constitution:

1. Preamble—The preamble is the introduction that explains the Constitution and the government it describes.

2. Articles—The seven articles explain the government's structure.

3. Amendments—The amendments are the changes to the original seven articles.

The Constitution has four basic principles:

1. There are three branches of government (executive, legislative, judicial) that separate and balance powers.

2. The Constitution is the supreme law of the land, meaning that no other laws come above it.

3. All people and all states are equal before the law, and each state must be democratic and respect the law of other states.

4. The Constitution can be changed according to the methods outlined in it.

The fourth principle says it is possible to change, or amend, the Constitution. In order to suggest a change, or amendment, the House and Senate must have a two-thirds vote, or two-thirds of the states must call for a national convention to consider the amendment. To add an amendment to the Constitution, three-fourths of the states must vote for it. There are currently 27 amendments.

The Constitution also explains how the office of president works. To be elected to that office, a person must be a natural-born citizen of the United States, be at least 35 years old, and have lived in the United States for at least 14 years. If the president dies before completing his or her term, the vice president becomes president. If the president and vice president die, the leader of the House of Representatives, also called the Speaker of the House, becomes president. An amendment added in 1951 puts a term limit on the office; presidents can serve a maximum of two terms.

Bill of Rights

After the Constitution was written, some states would not sign it unless it protected citizens' freedoms and limited the power of the federal government. Ten amendments were written to provide those protections. When they were added to the Constitution, all the states signed it. The 10 amendments are called the Bill of Rights.

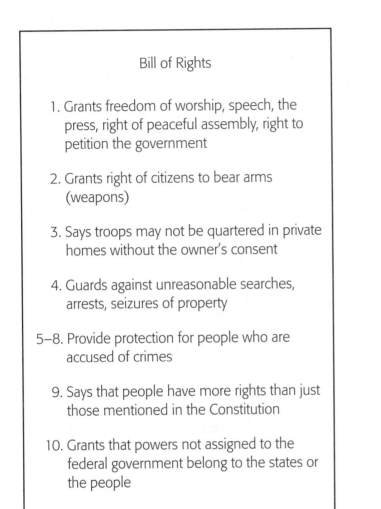

Bill of Rights

1. Grants freedom of worship, speech, the press, right of peaceful assembly, right to petition the government

2. Grants right of citizens to bear arms (weapons)

3. Says troops may not be quartered in private homes without the owner's consent

4. Guards against unreasonable searches, arrests, seizures of property

5–8. Provide protection for people who are accused of crimes

9. Says that people have more rights than just those mentioned in the Constitution

10. Grants that powers not assigned to the federal government belong to the states or the people

POLITICAL PARTIES

In the United States, many organizations can try to gain power by putting candidates in elections. These organizations are called political parties. There are two major parties that hold most elected offices and have the most registered voters as members: the Democratic party, which was founded in about 1828, and the Republican party, founded in 1854. Other parties that are currently active include the Libertarian Party, the Green Party, and the Constitution Party.

Voting in Elections

The right to vote in an American election has its own history. For hundreds of years, people were kept from voting for various reasons, including their gender, race, ability to read, land ownership, and income. Through a number of amendments to the Constitution, those reasons are now illegal. However in some states people who are serving time in prison, those who once committed a serious crime, and/or those with certain mental incapacities cannot vote.

To vote, you must be a United States citizen who is at least 18 years old. Before an election, you must register to vote by contacting your local election office, which is listed in the phonebook. Election offices are often called the county clerk's office or municipal board of elections. If you cannot find a listing, contact your state board of elections or check with your local library. A few weeks after registering, you should receive a notice in the mail that confirms your registration and tells you where to go to vote.

Pledge of Allegiance

The oath of allegiance to the country and its flag was written in 1892, and was changed twice before taking the form it has today. The word "flag" was changed to "flag of the United States of America" in 1924, and in 1954 the words "under God" were added. The Pledge, which is spoken with the right hand over the heart, is often recited at public events, and is currently required in the classrooms of 35 states.

THE PLEDGE OF ALLEGIANCE

I pledge allegiance to the Flag of the United States of America and to the Republic for which it stands, one nation, under God, indivisible, with liberty and justice for all.

Practice Questions

1. What is the Bill of Rights? _____

   _____

   _____

2. If the president dies, the _____
   becomes president.

3. To be eligible to vote, you must be at least _____ years old.

4. A president can serve for up to _____ terms.

5. Can all citizens of legal age vote? _____

6. The Constitution can be changed by adding a(n) _____

   _____.

7. What are three rights or freedoms guaranteed by the Bill of Rights?

   _____

   _____

   _____

8. The words _____
   were added to the Pledge of Allegiance in 1954.

9. Before you can vote, you need to _____.

10. A person must be at least _____ years of age to run for president.

Answers and Explanations

1. The first 10 amendments to the Constitution make up the Bill of Rights.

   Explanation: These amendments limit the power of the federal government and protect people's freedoms.

2. The vice president becomes president if the president dies.

   Explanation: The writers of the Constitution wanted to make sure that, if the president died, no individual or group would try to take over the government. They explained exactly what would happen if the president, and even the vice president died, so that there would be a smooth transition from one leader to another.

3. You must be at least 18 years of age to vote.

4. A president can serve two four-year terms.

   Explanation: After Franklin Roosevelt was elected to a fourth term, many Americans wanted term limits. They worried that a president could become too powerful if he or she served more than eight years, thus upsetting the balance of power and system of checks and balances.

5. No, not all citizens are allowed to vote.

   Explanation: Every citizen over the age of 18 is allowed to vote in most states. However, some states do not allow prisoners, former prisoners who committed serious crimes, and/or people with certain mental incapacities the right to vote.

6. The Constitution can be changed by adding an amendment.

7. The Bill of Rights guarantees freedom of worship, freedom of speech, and freedom of the press; the right of peaceful assembly, the right to petition the government, and the right to bear arms.

   Explanation: After the Constitution was written, some states would not sign it unless it provided protections for citizens against violations of their rights by the government, and limited the power of the federal government. Therefore, 10 amendments were added to secure these rights.

8. The words "under God" were added to the Pledge of Allegiance in 1954.

9. In order to vote, you must register.

10. Thirty-five is the minimum age one must be to run for president.

STEP 4 REVIEW

The following questions are similar to those you will have to answer during your USCIS interview.

Civics Practice Questions

Write the correct answer or circle the letter next to the correct answer choice.

1. The United States Supreme Court has _____ justices.

2. Why did the Pilgrims come to America? _____

   _____

   _____

3. The last states to be added to the United States were _____

   and _____.

4. Why wasn't the Jamestown colony successful?

   a. It did not have the help of Native Americans.

   b. Its tobacco crop failed.

   c. The settlers moved south after the first winter.

   d. It didn't have a good leader.

5. Who becomes the country's leader if the president is unable to complete his or her term? _____

_____

_____

6. When saying the Pledge of Allegiance, put your _____ hand over your heart.

7. What did most Southern states do when Abraham Lincoln was elected president?

_____

_____

_____

8. Segregation kept African Americans from being allowed to

a. register to vote.

b. hold government jobs.

c. attend schools with white children.

d. travel freely between states.

9. What was the Underground Railroad? _____

_____

_____

10. Who is the leader of the executive branch in local government? _____

_____

_____

11. The national anthem is _____

_____

_____.

12. One of America's allies during World War II was

    a. Japan.

    b. England.

    c. Italy.

    d. Germany.

13. What happened at Pearl Harbor? _____

_____

_____

14. What was the civil rights movement? _____

_____

_____

15. When a state was added, what happened to the stars and stripes on the flag?

_____

_____

_____

16. In which document did Thomas Jefferson write, "All men are created equal"?

    a. the Constitution

    b. the Bill of Rights

    c. the Declaration of Independence

    d. the Mayflower Compact

17. Can the Constitution be changed? _____

18. Who fought the Cold War? _____

_____

19. The two sides fighting the Civil War were called _____

and _____.

20. Who elects the President?

    a. the people

    b. the Senate

    c. the House of Representatives

    d. the Electoral College

ANSWERS AND EXPLANATIONS

1. Nine justices sit on the U.S. Supreme Court.

2. The Pilgrims came so they could freely practice their religion. The King of England did not allow the Pilgrims to practice their religion in that country.

3. Alaska and Hawaii were the last states to be added.

4. (a) The Jamestown colony was not successful because it did not have the help of Native Americans. The members of the Jamestown colony, unlike the Pilgrims in the colony at Plymouth, did not have a good relationship with the Native Americans living nearby.

5. In the event that the president is unable to finish his or her term, the vice president is next in line to become president.

6. When saying the Pledge of Allegiance, one should place the right hand over the heart.

7. They left the Union and formed the Confederate States of America.

   Explanation: Southern states held slaves, and they knew Abraham Lincoln was against slavery. They did not want to be ruled by someone who would try to take away their slaves, so they joined together and elected their own president.

8. (c) Segregation kept African Americans from being allowed to attend schools with white children.

    Explanation: Segregation meant that blacks and whites used separate facilities, including schools, public restrooms, and recreational facilities like pools.

9. The Underground Railroad was a system that helped Southern slaves escape to freedom in the North. However, it was neither underground nor a railroad. It was a number of different routes formed by Northerners, including freed slaves. Many people helped the slaves on these routes, hiding them and traveling with them until they reached a free state.

10. A mayor is the leader of local government. Citizens of towns and cities elect a mayor to lead their executive branch of government.

11. "The Star-Spangled Banner" is the national anthem.

12. (b) England and the United States were allies during World War II.

    Explanation: Japan, Italy, and Germany were enemies of the United States.

13. The Japanese bombed the U.S. Navy base there in 1941, provoking America to enter World War II. Until the bombing, the United States did not want to get involved with the war. After the attack, it declared war on Japan, and the next day Japan's allies, Germany and Italy, declared war on the United States.

14. The civil rights movement was a struggle for equality for African Americans. In 1955, Dr. Martin Luther King Jr. and his followers began protesting the unfair treatment of African Americans. During the 1960s, protests continued, including the March on Washington in 1963. Congress passed two civil rights bills, but problems continued.

15. A star was added, but the number of stripes remained the same. There are 50 stars on the flag, one for every state. The 13 stripes never changed—they represent the original 13 colonies.

16. (c) The Declaration of Independence, authored by Jefferson, declared that all people were equal and that the colonists deserved independence from England.

17. Yes, the Constitution can be changed by adding amendments. To suggest an amendment, the House and Senate must have a two-thirds vote, or two-thirds of the states must call for a national convention to consider the amendment. To add an amendment to the Constitution, three-fourths of the states must vote for it.

18. The Soviet Union and United States were the two superpowers that fought the Cold War.

    Explanation: Although it was called a war, there was no actual fighting during the Cold War. The superpowers made so many nuclear weapons that they knew they would destroy each other if they ever used them. This fear of destruction kept both countries from wanting to fight directly.

19. Confederate and Union, or South and North

20. (d) The Electoral College, made up of "electors" from each state, chooses the president. The electors' votes are based on the votes of citizens in the states they represent.

NOTES

_____

_____

_____

_____

_____

_____

_____

_____

_____

_____

_____

_____

_____

_____

_____

_____

_____

_____

_____

_____

_____

_____

_____

_____

_____

_____

_____

_____

_____

_____

_____

_____

_____

_____

_____

_____

_____

_____

_____

_____

_____

_____

_____

_____

_____

_____

_____

_____

_____

_____

_____

Step 5: **Take the English Communication Practice Test**

Remember that during your interview your ability to read, write, and speak English is tested. The following exercises help you practice these skills. If you encounter any unfamiliar words, write them down in the Notes section at the end of this chapter, or on a separate piece of paper, and look up their definitions using a dictionary or the Glossary at the end of this book.

PRACTICE QUESTIONS

Practice reading these sentences out loud:

1. The United States is the land of freedom.

2. I want to be an American citizen.

3. The first president was George Washington.

4. Congress meets in the Capitol.

5. The American flag is red, white, and blue.

6. Freedom is worth fighting for.

7. Congress can declare war.

8. Voting is very important.

9. The United States government has three branches.

10. Our capital is Washington, DC.

Write the answers to these questions in the space provided:

11. How many states are in the Union? _____

_____

_____

12. Where is the White House? _____

_____

_____

13. Who was Thomas Jefferson? _____

_____

_____

14. How many stripes are on the flag? _____

_____

_____

15. What is the national anthem?

_____

_____

16. Who was the first president? _____

_____

_____

17. What are the three branches of government? _____

_____

_____

18. Why did the United States enter World War II?_____

_____

_____

19. What major river that runs north to south divides the United States? ____

_____

_____

20. How long is one presidential term? _____

_____

_____

21. Who was Martha Washington? _____

_____

_____

22. What is the most important right granted to a U.S. citizen? _____

_____

_____

23. When is Independence Day? _____

_____

_____

24. How many justices are there on the Supreme Court? _____

_____

_____

25. What do we call the elected leader of a state? _____

_____

_____

26. What does the president's cabinet do? _____

_____

_____

27. Who was Thomas Edison? _____

_____

_____

28. What is the maximum number of terms that a president may be elected to?

_____

_____

_____

29. Who is the commander in chief of the United States military? _____

_____

_____

30. Who was president during the Civil War? _____

_____

_____

Read the passage and answer questions 31–35:

The Pilgrims left England in 1620 because they wanted religious freedom. They came to America on a ship called the Mayflower, and landed in Plymouth. The Pilgrims had a hard time getting used to their new land. The winter was very cold, and finding food was not easy. However, when the Pilgrims landed, there were already people living in the area. Tribes of Native Americans met with the Pilgrims and saw that they needed help. They taught the Pilgrims how to plant seeds, catch fish, and hunt for and gather food. To celebrate their first harvest, the Pilgrims invited the Native Americans for a meal, which we now celebrate every November as Thanksgiving.

31. Why did the Pilgrims leave England? _____

_____

_____

32. What was the name of their ship? _____

_____

_____

33. Who helped the Pilgrims in America? _____

_____

_____

34. What did Native Americans teach the Pilgrims? _____

_____

_____

35. What holiday was first celebrated in Plymouth? _____

_____

_____

Read and answer the following questions out loud:

36. Have you ever used other names?

37. Are you at least 18 years old?

38. What is your current marital status?

39. What is your mailing address?

40. Where have you lived during the last five years?

41. How many days did you spend outside the United States in the last five years?

42. If you are married, what is your spouse's name?

43. How many sons and daughters do you have?

44. Have you ever voted in a U.S. election?

45. Do you owe any overdue federal, state, or local taxes?

46. Have you ever been charged with committing a crime?

47. Have you ever served in the U.S. military?

48. When required by law, are you willing to bear arms for the United States?

49. Is your spouse a citizen of the United States?

50. Do you understand the oath of allegiance to the Untied States?

ANSWERS AND EXPLANATIONS

11. There are 50 states in the Union.

12. The White House is in Washington, DC (at 1600 Pennsylvania Avenue).

13. Thomas Jefferson was the main writer of the Declaration of Independence and the third president.

14. There are 13 stripes on the flag, representing the original 13 colonies.

15. "The Star-Spangled Banner" is the national anthem.

16. George Washington was the first president.

17. The three branches of government are the executive, legislative, and judicial.

18. The United States entered World War II because it was attacked by the Japanese at Pearl Harbor.

19. The Mississippi River runs north to south, dividing the United States.

20. One presidential term is four years.

KAPLAN

21. Martha Washington was the wife of the first president, George Washington.

22. The most important right of a United States citizen is the right to vote.

23. Independence Day is on July fourth.

24. There are nine Supreme Court justices.

25. The elected leader of a state is called a governor.

26. The president's cabinet gives him advice.

27. Thomas Edison was the inventor of the light bulb, among other inventions.

28. The maximum number of terms a president may serve is two four-year terms.

29. The president is the commander in chief of the United States military.

30. Abraham Lincoln was president during the Civil War.

31. The Pilgrims left England for religious freedom.

32. The Pilgrims's ship was the Mayflower.

33. Native Americans helped the Pilgrims.

34. Native Americans taught the Pilgrims how to plant seeds, hunt for and gather food, and catch fish.

35. Thanksgiving was first celebrated in Plymouth by the Pilgrims and Native Americans.

NOTES

_____

_____

_____

_____

_____

_____

_____

_____

_____

_____

_____

_____

_____

_____

_____

_____

_____

_____

_____

_____

_____

_____

_____

_____

_____

_____

_____

_____

_____

_____

_____

_____

_____

_____

_____

_____

_____

_____

_____

_____

_____

_____

_____

_____

_____

_____

_____

_____

_____

_____

_____

_____

_____

_____

_____

_____

_____

_____

_____

_____

_____

Step 6: **Take the Civics Practice Test**

SHORT-ANSWER QUESTIONS

1. Who helped the Pilgrims when they landed in Plymouth? _____

    _____

    _____

2. Why did the United States enter World War II? _____

    _____

    _____

3. What was the Emancipation Proclamation? _____

    _____

    _____

4. Why are there 50 stars on the American flag? _____

    _____

    _____

KAPLAN

5. What are some of the reasons immigrants came to America? _____

    _____

    _____

6. How did plantations in the South produce so much cotton and tobacco?

    _____

    _____

    _____

7. What was the Cold War? _____

    _____

    _____

8. What is the main idea of the Declaration of Independence? _____

    _____

    _____

9. What was the Boston Tea Party?_____

    _____

    _____

10. Who was Dr. Martin Luther King Jr.? _____

    _____

    _____

11. What does "checks and balances" mean? _____

_____

_____

12. Who helped America recover from the Great Depression? _____

_____

_____

13. Who fought the Civil War? _____

_____

_____

14. What was the Louisiana Purchase? _____

_____

_____

15. Why did the colonists fight the Revolutionary War? _____

_____

_____

16. Why does California have more representatives in the federal House of Representatives than Vermont does?

_____

_____

_____

17. What was the Underground Railroad? _____

_____

_____

18. How did the Cold War end? _____

_____

_____

19. Why was George Washington the first commander in chief of the U.S. military?

_____

_____

_____

20. For how long do Supreme Court justices serve? _____

_____

_____

21. When is Independence Day? _____

_____

_____

22. Why is America called a melting pot? _____

_____

_____

23. Why did Patrick Henry say, "Give me liberty or give me death"? _____

_____

_____

24. Why did the United States enter World War I? _____

_____

_____

25. What was Reconstruction? _____

_____

_____

26. What is the supreme law of the land? _____

_____

_____

27. What group of people advises the president? _____

_____

_____

28. How did the Civil War improve the lives of African Americans? _____

_____

_____

29. What was the suffrage movement? _____

_____

_____

30. How are laws passed? _____

_____

_____

31. Can court decisions be overturned? _____

_____

_____

32. What was the League of Nations? _____

_____

_____

33. Why is the War of 1812 called the Second War of Independence? _____

_____

_____

34. What was the Continental Congress? _____

_____

_____

35. Why are there 13 stripes on the flag? _____

_____

_____

36. What is the Iron Curtain? _____

_____

_____

37. How did the colonists gain independence from England? _____

_____

_____

38. What was the Confederate States of America? _____

_____

_____

39. What is segregation? _____

_____

_____

40. What is the United Nations? _____

_____

_____

41. Why did the writers of the Bill of Rights want to guarantee freedom of religion?

   _____

   _____

   _____

42. Does every bill that gets a majority vote in Congress become a law? ____

   _____

   _____

43. How are state governments organized? _____

   _____

   _____

44. What are the three parts of the Constitution? _____

   _____

   _____

45. What famous landmark did immigrants pass on their way to Ellis Island?

   _____

   _____

   _____

46. What is one reason the Native Americans could not successfully negotiate with and defend themselves from European settlers?

_____

_____

_____

47. Who was Thomas Jefferson? _____

_____

_____

48. What was the March on Washington? _____

_____

_____

49. Who was John F. Kennedy? _____

_____

_____

50. What is one way in which Congress can have some control over the executive branch?

_____

_____

_____

ANSWERS AND EXPLANATIONS

1. Native Americans helped the Pilgrims.

   Explanation: When the Pilgrims landed in Plymouth, they did not know what to expect. They did not know where to find food, what types of seeds they could grow, or how to live through harsh winters. Tribes of Native Americans living in the area showed the Pilgrims how to survive.

2. The Japanese bombed Pearl Harbor.

   Explanation: America did not want to enter World War II, but the Japanese bombed the U.S. Navy base in Pearl Harbor in 1941, and America declared war on them. The next day, Japan's allies, Germany and Italy, declared war on the United States, and the world was once again at war.

3. The Emancipation Proclamation was an order issued by President Lincoln to free slaves in the 11 confederate states.

   Explanation: The confederate states were fighting the Civil War to keep their slaves. Lincoln believed if they had to free their slaves, they would stop fighting.

4. There is one star for every state.

   Explanation: The flag began with 13 stars, representing the original 13 colonies. As states were added to the Union, additional stars were added. Hawaii and Alaska were the last two states added, bringing the total to 50 stars.

5. Immigrants came for many reasons, including religious freedom and opportunity; and to escape war, persecution, famine, and poverty.

    Explanation: Immigrants have been coming to America since colonial times, because they believe it gives them the chance to have better lives than the ones they led in their native countries. That could mean being able to practice their religion freely, to get a better job, or to live in peace.

6. They used slaves to produce the cotton and tobacco.

    Explanation: The Southern states' use of slave labor allowed them to grow enough cotton and tobacco to meet the demand, and to make huge profits.

7. The Cold War was a "war" between the Soviet Union and the United States that did not involve actual fighting.

    Explanation: The two enemies had an arms race, meaning they made more and better weapons to fight one another. But those weapons were so powerful that the countries were afraid to use them, so they never fought each other.

8. All men are created equal.

    Explanation: Thomas Jefferson wrote "all men are created equal" as part of his argument that the colonists had the right to form their own government and be independent from England.

9. The Boston Tea Party was a protest by colonists against the taxes England was making them pay.

    Explanation: The English collected many taxes from the colonists, which made the colonists angry. They protested by boycotting, and sometimes destroying, English products. When a ship full of English tea came to Boston, colonists boarded the ship and dumped the tea into the water.

10. Dr. Martin Luther King Jr. was a leader in the civil rights movement.

   Explanation: In the 1950s and 1960s, African Americans began to protest the way they were being treated. As the protests grew, Dr. King became a leader who helped organize them and speak out against injustice.

11. The three branches of government keep power separated and balanced, and the branches oversee one another so no branch becomes too powerful.

   Explanation: The writers of the Constitution did not want someone who had too much power to lead America, so they divided that power into three branches.

12. President Roosevelt started programs called the New Deal to end the Great Depression in America.

   Explanation: Roosevelt's New Deal included programs to create jobs, reopen banks and businesses, and start Social Security.

13. The Southern states fought the Northern states.

   Explanation: When Abraham Lincoln became president, 11 Southern states left the Union because they wanted to keep their slaves, and Lincoln and the Northern states wanted them freed. The Southern states formed their own country and attacked the North, beginning the Civil War.

14. President Thomas Jefferson bought the Louisiana Territory from France.

   Explanation: Jefferson's purchase doubled the size of the country, and made westward expansion possible.

15. The colonists wanted to gain independence from England.

    Explanation: After over 100 years of English rule, the colonists wanted to govern themselves. The fighting began when English soldiers tried to take weapons from the Massachusetts colonists, and the colonists attacked them.

16. The number of representatives is based on population.

    Explanation: Although each state has two senators in the senate, the 435 seats in the House of Representatives are divided according to how many people live in each state. California has 53 representatives, and Vermont has one.

17. The Underground Railroad was a way for Southern slaves to escape to freedom in the North.

    Explanation: During the Civil War, many Northerners spoke out and wrote against slavery, and some helped slaves to escape to the North where they were free.

18. Russia was no longer a superpower; it had an improved relationship with the United States, and the two countries agreed to reduce weapons.

    Explanation: Two Soviet leaders signed treaties with the United States to limit nuclear weapons. After the second treaty was signed, the Soviet Union fell apart and was divided into four countries.

19. Because the president is also the commander in chief.

    Explanation: The Constitution explains the powers of the president, and makes him commander in chief of the military. Because George Washington was the first president, he was also the first commander in chief.

KAPLAN

20. Supreme Court justices serve until they want to retire.

   Explanation: Supreme Court Justices have no term limit, which means that after the president appoints them and they are confirmed, they are said to have a lifetime appointment.

21. Independence Day is July fourth.

   Explanation: The Declaration of Independence was adopted on July 4, 1776. That day is now celebrated as Independence Day.

22. Because immigrants from many different countries live here together.

   Explanation: Although immigrant groups came here with different languages, cultures, and customs, they blended, or "melted," together to form one country.

23. Because he wanted to convince his fellow Virginian colonists to fight in the Revolutionary War.

   Explanation: Many of the Virginia colonists were loyalists, meaning they were loyal to the king of England. They did not believe the colonies should become an independent country. Patrick Henry's speech convinced them to send troops from Virginia to fight in the Revolutionary War.

24. German submarines attacked U.S. ships in the Atlantic Ocean.

   Explanation: America did not want to get involved in the war in Europe that had England, France, Russia, and Italy fighting the Germans. However, the Germans attacked our ships and we declared war on them.

25. The period of time after the Civil War.

    Explanation: When the war was over, the United States had to "reconstruct," or rebuild itself. The Southern states that had left before the war rejoined the Union.

26. The supreme law of the land is the Constitution.

    Explanation: The Constitution established the court system, the Congress, and the presidency, including an explanation of how to select the president and the qualifications needed for the position.

27. The cabinet is the group that advises the president.

    Explanation: The cabinet is made up of the vice president; attorney general; secretary of state; heads of government agencies such as the Department of Defense, Department of the Treasury, and Department of Homeland Security; as well as other officials the president chooses.

28. The Civil War brought an end to slavery.

    Explanation: In the South, many laws were passed after the war that made life very difficult for African Americans. Even though they were no longer slaves, they were mostly poor, uneducated, and unable to make changes in their situation.

29. The suffrage movement was a fight for women's right to vote.

    Explanation: Most states did not allow women the right to vote, and suffragists protested for many years to gain that right. They succeeded in 1920, when the Nineteenth Amendment was added to the Constitution.

30. Laws are passed when they get a majority vote in Congress.

    Explanation: Senators and representatives introduce bills, which are proposals for laws. If a bill wins a vote in the Senate and the House, it becomes a law.

31. Higher courts can overturn the decisions made by lower courts.

    Explanation: The judicial branch is set up so that defendants can appeal to higher courts to reconsider the decisions made by lower courts. The Supreme Court is the highest court in the country.

32. The League of Nations was an international organization formed after World War I that worked to prevent another war.

    Explanation: President Wilson suggested the league during the signing of the peace treaty that ended World War I.

33. In the War of 1812, we fought the same country that we won independence from 30 years before.

    Explanation: Even after granting independence to the colonists, England still wanted control. It invaded the United States in 1812, and was defeated two years later at the Battle of New Orleans. With that defeat, America became truly independent.

34. The Continental Congress was a group of representatives from the original colonies who wrote and adopted the Declaration of Independence.

    Explanation: The Continental Congress first met to organize a protest against England. When the king refused to meet their demands, they decided they should seek independence.

35. The stripes represent the original 13 colonies.

    Explanation: The flag began with 13 stripes and 13 stars. While the number of stars grew each time a state was added, the number of stripes stayed the same.

36. The Iron Curtain referred to the line between the Soviet Union and the rest of Europe.

    Explanation: After World War II, Communist Russia took over many surrounding countries, forming the Soviet Union. The people of the Soviet Union were not allowed to leave, and there was almost no contact between the Soviet Union and the rest of Europe, leading many to describe the line separating the two as an Iron Curtain—one through which nothing could pass.

37. The colonists gained independence by winning the Revolutionary War.

    Explanation: Although the Declaration of Independence was signed on July 4, 1776, England did not recognize the United States as an independent country until it lost the war in 1781.

38. The Confederate States of America was the name 11 slave states chose after leaving the Union.

    Explanation: When Abraham Lincoln was elected president, most slave states decided to form their own country. They elected Jefferson Davis as their president. The states rejoined the Union after the Civil War, bringing an end to the Confederacy.

39. Segregation is the practice of separating people by race.

   Explanation: African Americans were equal by law, but laws requiring segregation kept them from enjoying equality in the Southern states. For example, they could not go to school, live in the same neighborhoods, or swim in the same pools with whites.

40. The United Nations is an organization that was formed to promote world peace.

   Explanation: After World War II, the failure of the League of Nations to keep the peace was obvious. Fifty-one countries came together to create a new organization that would take its place and work to solve differences between countries to prevent them from going to war.

41. Freedom of religion was important to the writers of the Bill of Rights because many of America's first settlers came here to be able to practice their religion freely. The countries they came from, including England, did not allow this freedom.

42. No; the president can reject (veto) bills passed by Congress so they do not become laws.

   Explanation: The Constitution explains the president's veto power. It is part of the system of checks and balances because it helps prevent Congress from becoming too powerful. In this way, the president checks Congress's power.

43. State governments are generally set up like the federal government, with three branches.

   Explanation: A state legislative branch typically has a Senate and House of Representatives, and its judicial branch is made up of a series of courts, headed by a State Supreme Court. The head of the executive branch is the governor.

44. The Constitution is made up of the preamble, articles, and amendments.

    Explanation: The preamble is an introduction that explains the purpose of the Constitution and the government it describes. The seven articles detail how the government is structured. The amendments are changes to the original Constitution.

45. Immigrants passed the Statue of Liberty on their way to Ellis Island.

    Explanation: The statue became a symbol of welcome to the millions of people seeking a new life in America.

46. The many tribes were very different, and they were geographically separated from one another.

    Explanation: The tribes had their own languages; styles of clothing and shelter; and methods of hunting, growing, and preparing food. The tribes were spread across the country, making it difficult for them to organize. Because some were enemies of other tribes, it was not easy to fight for a common goal.

47. Thomas Jefferson was the third president, and the main writer of the Declaration of Independence.

    Explanation: Jefferson's ideas and abilities made him a leader of early America. He is known as one of the Founding Fathers.

48. The March on Washington was a civil rights movement protest held in 1963.

    Explanation: The march was the largest political protest in U.S. history at the time it was held. Over 200,000 people attended the event, which ended with Dr. Martin Luther King Jr.'s famous "I have a dream" speech.

49. John F. Kennedy was president during the early 1960s.

    Explanation: Kennedy was a supporter of Dr. Martin Luther King Jr., and helped the civil rights movement by proposing a Civil Rights Bill to Congress. Congress passed the bill, six months after the president was assassinated.

50. Congress can choose not to approve a president's treaties and nominations for positions such as judges. Congress can also impeach a president.

    Explanation: The Congress gets these powers from the Constitution to ensure that no one branch can ever have complete control.

NOTES

_____

_____

_____

_____

_____

_____

_____

_____

_____

_____

_____

_____

_____

_____

_____

_____

_____

_____

_____

_____

_____

_____

100 Frequently Asked U.S. History and Government Questions and Answers

These questions, which were adapted from the U.S. Citizen and Immigration Services website (www.uscis.gov), are typical of those asked during the naturalization exam.

1. When is Independence Day celebrated? _____

   _____

   _____

2. From what country did America become independent? _____

   _____

   _____

3. How many senators are there in Congress? _____

   _____

   _____

4. How long is the term of a U.S. Supreme Court justice? _____

   _____

   _____

5. Who made the first U.S. flag? _____

    _____

    _____

6. How many representatives are in the House of Representatives?

    _____

    _____

7. How long is a representative's term? _____

    _____

    _____

8. Which president freed the slaves? _____

    _____

    _____

9. What did the Emancipation Proclamation do? _____

    _____

    _____

10. What is the capital of your state? _____

    _____

    _____

11. Which president is called the "Father of our Country"? _____

_____

_____

12. What special group advises the president? _____

_____

_____

13. In what year was the Constitution written? _____

_____

_____

14. What are the first 10 amendments to the Constitution called? _____

_____

_____

15. What colors are on the American flag? _____

_____

_____

16. Who are your state's two senators? _____

_____

_____

17. How long is a senator's term? _____

_____

_____

18. What are Congress's duties? _____

_____

_____

19. Which president was the first commander in chief of the U.S. military?

_____

_____

_____

20. Can the Constitution be changed? _____

_____

_____

21. How many stars are on the American flag? _____

_____

_____

22. What country did the colonists fight in the Revolutionary War? _____

_____

_____

23. Who was the first president of the United States? _____

_____

_____

24. In what month does the country vote for the president? _____

_____

_____

25. Who is in the executive branch? _____

_____

_____

26. Name three of the rights or freedoms guaranteed by the Bill of Rights.

_____

_____

_____

27. Who has the power to declare war? _____

_____

_____

28. What kind of government does the United States have? _____

_____

_____

29. Who elects the members of Congress? _____

_____

_____

30. What color are the stars on the American flag? _____

_____

_____

31. What is a change to the Constitution called? _____

_____

_____

32. What U.S. Citizenship and Immigration Services (USCIS) form is used to apply for naturalized citizenship?

_____

_____

_____

33. Who helped the Pilgrims in America? _____

_____

_____

34. On what ship did the Pilgrims come to America? _____

_____

_____

35. What were the 13 original states of the United States called before obtaining their independence from England? _____

_____

_____

36. Who is in the judicial branch? _____

_____

_____

37. Name one purpose of the United Nations. _____

_____

_____

38. Where does Congress meet? _____

_____

_____

39. Whose rights are guaranteed by the Constitution and the Bill of Rights?

_____

_____

_____

40. What do the stars on the American flag represent? _____

_____

_____

41. Who is your state's governor? _____

_____

_____

42. How many Constitutional amendments are there? _____

_____

_____

43. What is the introduction to the Constitution called? _____

_____

_____

44. Name one benefit of being a citizen of the United States. _____

_____

_____

45. What is the most important right granted to U.S. citizens? _____

_____

_____

46. Who elects the president of the United States? _____

_____

_____

47. What are the Supreme Court's duties? _____

_____

_____

48. In what month is the newly elected president inaugurated? _____

_____

_____

49. How many times can a senator be re-elected? _____

_____

_____

50. How many stripes are on the American flag? _____

_____

_____

51. Who leads your local government? _____

_____

_____

52. If the president dies, who becomes president of the United States?

_____

_____

53. How many branches are in the government? _____

_____

_____

54. How many times can a congressperson be re-elected? _____

_____

_____

55. Why did the Pilgrims come to America? _____

_____

_____

56. What two political parties are the major parties in the United States?

_____

_____

_____

57. If the president and the vice president die, who becomes president of the
United States?

_____

_____

_____

58. What is the supreme law of the United States? _____

_____

_____

59. How many states are there in the United States? _____

_____

_____

60. What colors are the stripes on the American flag? _____

_____

_____

61. What is the most important belief of the Declaration of Independence?

_____

_____

62. What is one of the requirements a person must meet to be eligible to become president, according to the Constitution?

_____

_____

_____

63. What year did the Civil War begin? _____

_____

_____

64. What are the three branches of the government? _____

_____

_____

65. How old must you be in order to vote in the United States? _____

_____

_____

66. Who is the head of a state government? _____

_____

_____

67. What states were the 49th and 50th to join the Union? _____

_____

_____

68. How long is the president's term? _____

_____

_____

69. What is the Bill of Rights? _____

_____

_____

70. What do the stripes on the American flag represent? _____

_____

_____

71. What is the name of the president's official home? _____

    _____

    _____

72. What is the national anthem? _____

    _____

    _____

73. Why are there 100 senators in the Senate? _____

    _____

    _____

74. What are the 13 original states? _____

    _____

    _____

75. What are the responsibilities of the legislative branch? _____

    _____

    _____

76. Who signs bills into law? _____

    _____

    _____

77. Who is the head of a city government? _____

   _____

   _____

78. The president can serve how many terms? _____

   _____

   _____

79. What is the Constitution? _____

   _____

   _____

80. How many states are there in the United States of America? _____

   _____

   _____

81. What is one of the rights guaranteed by the First Amendment? _____

   _____

   _____

82. Who is the U.S. military's commander in chief? _____

   _____

   _____

83. Who wrote "The Star-Spangled Banner"? _____

_____

_____

84. Who selects the Supreme Court justices? _____

_____

_____

85. Who said, "Give me liberty or give me death"? _____

_____

_____

86. Who can make laws? _____

_____

_____

87. What is the United States' highest court? _____

_____

_____

88. The American colonists celebrated what holiday for the first time? _____

_____

_____

89. Who was Martin Luther King Jr.? _____

_____

_____

90. What is the Fourth of July? _____

_____

_____

91. What is the capital of the United States? _____

_____

_____

92. What is the White House? _____

_____

_____

93. Where is the White House? _____

_____

_____

94. Where does freedom of speech come from? _____

_____

_____

95. How many Supreme Court justices are there? _____

_____

_____

96. During World War II, which countries were our enemies? _____

_____

_____

97. What is Congress? _____

_____

_____

98. Who was the president during the Civil War? _____

_____

_____

99. Who was the lead writer of the Declaration of Independence?

_____

_____

100. When was the Declaration of Independence adopted?

_____

_____

ANSWERS

1. July Fourth

2. England

3. 100

4. Once appointed to the court, a U.S. Supreme Court justice serves on the court for life.

5. Betsy Ross

6. 435

7. two years

8. Abraham Lincoln

9. freed many slaves

10. varies by state

11. George Washington

12. the cabinet

13. 1787

14. the Bill of Rights

15. red, white, and blue

16. varies by state

17. six years

18. to make laws

19. George Washington

20. yes

21. 50

22. England

23. George Washington

24. November

25. the president, cabinet, and departments under the cabinet members

26. The rights included in the Bill of Rights are as follows:

(1) The right of freedom of speech, press, religion, peaceable assembly, and requesting change of government

(2) The right to bear arms (the right to have weapons or own a gun, though subject to certain regulations)

(3) The government may not quarter, or house, soldiers in the people's homes during peacetime without the people's consent

(4) The government may not search or take a person's property without a warrant

(5) A person may not be tried twice for the same crime and does not have to testify against himself

(6) A person charged with a crime still has some rights, such as the right to a lawyer and a trial

(7) The right to trial by jury in most cases

(8) Protects people against excessive or unreasonable fines or cruel and unusual punishment

(9) The people have rights other than those mentioned in the Constitution

(10) Any power not given to the federal government by the Constitution is a power of either the state or the people

27. Congress

28. Republican

29. the people; voters in each state

30. white

31. amendment

32. Form N-400, Application to File Petition for Naturalization

33. Native Americans; American Indians

34. the Mayflower

35. colonies

36. the Supreme Court

37. as a forum for countries to discuss and try to resolve world problems; to provide economic aid to many countries

38. in the Capitol in Washington, DC

39. everyone living in the United States—citizens and noncitizens

40. one for every state

41. varies by state

42. 27

43. the preamble

44. get federal government jobs; travel with a U.S. passport; petition for close relatives to come to the United States to live

45. the right to vote

46. the Electoral College

47. to interpret the Constitution and review laws

48. January

49. no limit

50. 13

51. varies by city or town

52. the vice president

53. three

54. no limit

55. for religious freedom

56. Democratic and Republican

57. Speaker of the House of Representatives

58. the Constitution

59. 50

60. red and white

61. all men are created equal

62. must be a natural born citizen of the United States; must be at least 35 years old by the time he/she will serve; must have lived in the United States for at least 14 years

63. 1861

64. executive, legislative, and judicial

65. 18

66. governor

67. Hawaii and Alaska

68. four years

69. the first 10 amendments of the Constitution

70. the original 13 states

71. the White House

72. "The Star-Spangled Banner"

73. two from each state

74. Connecticut, Delaware, Georgia, Maryland, Massachusetts, New Hampshire, New Jersey, New York, North Carolina, Pennsylvania, Rhode Island, South Carolina, and Virginia

75. Congress

76. the president

77. mayor

78. two four-year terms

79. the supreme law of the land; a document that explains our form of
government and its laws

80. 50

81. freedom of: speech, press, religion, peaceable assembly, and requesting
change of the government

82. the president

83. Francis Scott Key

84. Appointed by the president

85. Patrick Henry

86. Congress

87. the Supreme Court

88. Thanksgiving

89. a leader in the civil rights movement

90. Independence Day

91. the building in which Congress meets

92. the president's home while serving his or her term

93. Washington, DC (1600 Pennsylvania Avenue, NW)

94. the Bill of Rights

95. nine

96. Germany, Italy, and Japan

97. the Senate and the House of Representatives

98. Abraham Lincoln

99. Thomas Jefferson

100. July 4, 1776

NOTES

_____

_____

_____

_____

_____

_____

_____

_____

_____

_____

_____

_____

_____

_____

_____

_____

_____

Glossary

Many of these terms are found on Form N-400, and on the English and Civics tests during your interview. Be sure you understand each one; use a dictionary to find the definitions of new words, and study those that are not familiar to you.

allegiance—Loyalty to a nation. When you say the Pledge of Allegiance, you promise to be loyal to the United States.

allies—Countries that fight a war on the same side. Our allies during World War I were England and France. In World War II, our allies were Russia, England, and France.

amendment—A change to the Constitution. Currently there are 27 amendments.

Atlantic Ocean—The body of water on the east coast of the United States.

Bill of Rights—The first 10 amendments to the Constitution, which protect individuals' freedoms and limit the power of the federal government.

Boston Tea Party—A protest by colonists against the taxes England was making them pay.

cabinet—The president's advisors.

Capitol building—The place where Congress meets in Washington, DC.

checks and balances—Provided by separating the power of the federal government into three branches; each branch can "check" on the others to make sure they are working the way they are supposed to, and that power is balanced among all three.

citizen—Someone who by birth or naturalization owes loyalty to a country and is protected by it.

Civil Rights Amendment—The Fourteenth Amendment, passed after the Civil War, which gave African Americans full rights as citizens.

Civil War—The conflict between Northern free states and Southern slave states fought from 1861—1865.

Cold War—The "war" between the Soviet Union and the United States that was never fought directly.

Confederate States of America—The name given to 11 slave-holding states that left the Union when Lincoln was elected. The president of the Confederacy was Jefferson Davis.

Congress—The legislative branch of the federal government that makes laws. Congress is made up of the House of Representatives and the Senate.

Constitution—The document that explains our laws, our government, and the powers of the government. It is also called the supreme law of the land.

continuous residence—The length of time a permanent resident lives in the United States without taking a long trip out of the country. Most people who apply for naturalization need five years of continuous residence.

Declaration of Independence—The document that explained to England that the colonies wanted to rule themselves. It was written mainly by Thomas Jefferson and adopted by the colonies on July 4, 1776.

Edison, Thomas—The famous American inventor of the light bulb and other inventions.

Electoral College—A group of electors from each state that officially chooses the president about a month after the general election in November.

Ellis Island—A place in New York Harbor where, between 1892 and 1954, over 12 million immigrants landed before being admitted into the United States.

Emancipation Proclamation—An order issued by President Lincoln during the Civil War to free slaves in the 11 confederate states.

England—The country where the first colonists came from, and which ruled the colonists until it was defeated in the Revolutionary War.

executive branch—Headed by the president, the branch of the federal government that carries out laws, commands the armed forces, and directs foreign policy.

Father of our Country—The name given to the first president, George Washington.

fingerprint—An impression of the fingertip made in ink. Fingerprints are taken after you file Form N-400, the Application for Naturalization. They are used for identification because no two people's fingerprints are alike.

Form N-400—The Application for Naturalization.

freedom of the press—A right guaranteed to American citizens by the Bill of Rights; it states that the federal government cannot control the press, or media.

freedom of religion—A right guaranteed to American citizens by the Bill of Rights stating that citizens can practice any (or no) religion without interference by the federal government.

freedom of speech—A right guaranteed to American citizens by the Bill of Rights ensuring that citizens can say or write their opinions without interference by the federal government.

free states—States that did not allow slavery. Most free states were in the North, and fought in the Union army during the Civil War.

governor—The elected head of a state.

Great Depression—The time during which the United States economy was very weak, beginning with the stock market crash of 1929 and ending with the New Deal programs of President Franklin Roosevelt.

Henry, Patrick—The Virginia colonist who inspired his colony to go to war with a famous speech in which he declared, "Give me liberty or give me death."

House of Representatives—Part of Congress; made up of 435 elected representatives who serve two-year terms. The state's population determines the number of representatives the state has in the House.

immigrant—Someone who leaves one country to live in another.

Independence Day—The holiday celebrating America's independence from England, celebrated each year on July fourth.

interview—A meeting with someone from the USCIS after you file form N-400. In the interview, you go over your application and take the English and Civics tests.

Iron Curtain—The Cold War term referring to the line between Communist countries in Eastern Europe and Democratic ones in the West.

Jamestown—The first English colony located in what is now Virginia.

Jefferson, Thomas—The third president and main writer of the Declaration of Independence.

Johnson, Andrew—Abraham Lincoln's vice president, who became president after Lincoln's assassination. He was in office during the period after the Civil War known as Reconstruction.

judicial branch—The part of the government that interprets the Constitution. It is made up of the court system, including the Supreme Court.

July fourth—The day Americans celebrate the country's independence from England.

Kennedy, John F.—The president during the civil rights movement in the early 1960s.

King Jr., Dr. Martin Luther—A leader in the civil rights movement.

League of Nations—A group of countries that came together after World War I to prevent another world war.

legislative branch—The part of the government that makes laws. It includes the Senate and House of Representatives.

Lincoln, Abraham—The president during the Civil War; he freed the slaves.

Louisiana Purchase—The land deal in which President Jefferson bought the Louisiana Territory from France, doubling the size of the United States.

March on Washington—The largest political protest in U.S. history at the time it was held (1963). Over 200,000 people attended the event, which ended with Dr. Martin Luther King Jr.'s famous "I have a dream" speech.

Mayflower—The boat used by the Pilgrims to come to America.

mayor—The elected head of a city or town.

melting pot—The name given to the United States referring to the fact that it brings together immigrants from many different countries.

Mississippi River—The body of water flowing north to south that divides the United States.

moral character—The kind of person you are. To be eligible for citizenship, you must be of good moral character. If you committed a certain type of crime, you may not be eligible to become a citizen.

Native Americans—People who were already living in America when the colonists landed.

naturalization—The way an immigrant becomes a citizen of the United States.

naturalization oath ceremony—After your application is accepted, you take the oath of allegiance and become a United States citizen.

New Deal—Government programs started by President Franklin Roosevelt to end the Great Depression in America.

Nineteenth Amendment—The 1920 change to the Constitution giving women the right to vote.

oath—A promise. When you say the oath of allegiance to the United States, you promise to renounce foreign allegiances, support the Constitution, and serve the United States.

Pacific Ocean—The body of water on the west coast of the United States.

passport—A government document that proves citizenship and allows you to travel to other countries.

Pearl Harbor—An American military base bombed by the Japanese in 1941. The next day, the United States entered World War II.

permanent resident—Someone who has permanent resident status according to immigration law. He or she has a permanent resident card. After five years, a permanent resident can apply for naturalization.

Pilgrim—A Protestant who left England to have religious freedom.

Pledge of Allegiance—A promise said by Americans showing loyalty to the flag and "the republic for which it stands."

Plymouth—The area in what is now Massachusetts where the pilgrims landed.

preamble—The introduction or first part of the Constitution.

Reagan, Ronald—The president during the end of the Cold War.

Reconstruction—The time of rebuilding after the Civil War. Southern states made it very difficult for freed slaves by taking away their rights.

republic—The kind of government we have in the United States.

Revolutionary War—The war fought by the colonists against England to gain their independence.

right to bear arms—A guarantee of American citizens given in the Bill of Rights.

Roosevelt, Franklin—The president who served four terms beginning in 1933. His New Deal programs helped America recover from the Great Depression.

segregation—The practice of separating black and white Americans, and denying blacks the same opportunities as whites had.

Senate—The part of Congress made up of 100 senators (two from each state) who serve six-year terms.

slave states—States where it was legal to own slaves until the Civil War. Slave states were in the South, and left the Union when Lincoln was elected, forming the Confederate States of America. They fought against the free states in the Civil War, lost the war, and once again became part of the Union.

"Star-Spangled Banner"—The national anthem, written by Francis Scott Key in 1814.

Supreme Court—The highest court in the United States, made up of nine justices who are appointed by the president to lifetime terms.

supreme law of the land—The Constitution.

term limit—The restriction on the number of years a president can serve (two terms).

Thanksgiving—A holiday first celebrated by the Pilgrims and Native Americans after their first successful harvest.

13 colonies—The original group that came together to declare independence from England and form the United States of America.

Underground Railroad—A system that helped slaves in the South escape to freedom, in which people guided and hid the slaves until they reached a free state.

United Nations—A group of countries that came together after World War II to try to prevent more wars and to give aid to poorer countries.

United States Citizenship and Immigration Services (USCIS)—The government agency that helps immigrants become citizens.

veto—The president's power to refuse to sign a bill into law.

War of 1812—America's "second war of independence" against England.

Washington, George—The first president of the United States.

Washington, Martha—The wife of the first president, George Washington.

White House—The home of the president and his or her family. The White House is at 1600 Pennsylvania Avenue in Washington, DC.

Wilson, Woodrow—The president during World War I who came up with the idea for the League of Nations.

World War I—The conflict between allies including France, England, Russia, Italy, and the United States and their enemies, including Germany. The United States entered the war after Germany destroyed an American submarine.

World War II—The conflict between allies including France, England, and the United States and their enemies Germany, Italy, and Japan. The United States entered World War II after Japan bombed its naval base in Pearl Harbor.

NOTES